VERA BRADLEY

OUR FAVORITE RECIPES

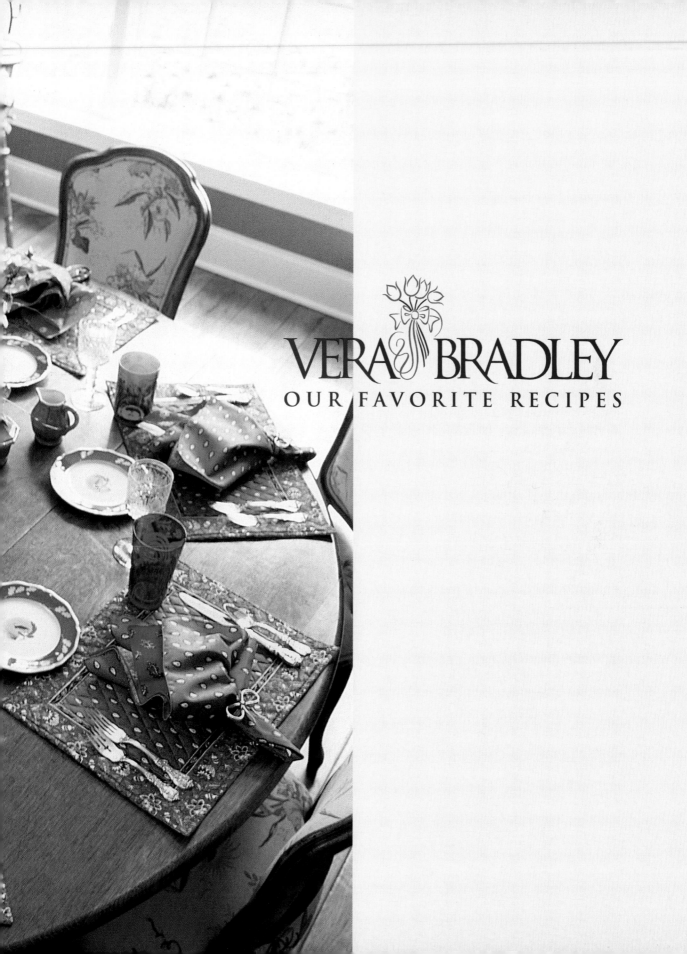

VERA BRADLEY
OUR FAVORITE RECIPES

VERA BRADLEY
OUR FAVORITE RECIPES

Published by Vera Bradley Designs, Inc.
Copyright© 2000 by
VERA BRADLEY DESIGNS, INC.
2208 Production Road
Fort Wayne, Indiana 46808

This cookbook is a collection of
favorite recipes, which are not
necessarily original recipes.

Edited, designed, and manufactured
in the United States of America by
Favorite Recipes® Press, an imprint of

FRP

P.O. Box 305142
Nashville, Tennessee 37230
800-358-0560

Book Design: Brad Whitfield and
    Susan Breining
Art Director: Steve Newman
Illustrator: Joanie Byrne Hall,
    Granddaughter of Vera Bradley
Project Manager: Linda A. Jones

Library of Congress Catalog Number:
00-091478
ISBN: 0-9679081-0-8
Manufactured in the
United States of America
First Printing: 2000   25,000 copies

INTRODUCTION

Friend by friend, our family has grown... likewise, special moments
and a shared love of camaraderie and good food have grown into this cookbook.
After years of sifting through piles of photocopied and e-mailed recipes,
our company thought it was finally time to take pen to paper and write our own
"culinary memoirs." Food just seems to be a natural part of our celebrations and
we're never short on snacks or coffee break goodies around the home office.
We've always thought that we'd make excellent caterers, if we didn't love
creating our handbags, luggage, and accessories so much!
This is a collection of recipes gathered from our family, friends, Vera Bradley
employees, representatives, and retailers—some amateur and some
professional chefs. Over *four hundred* recipes arrived at our doorstep which,
unfortunately, we had to narrow down to two hundred for print.
Difficult as this was, it was one of the tastiest tasks we ever had to do!
Each and every submission was tasted (sometimes five or six times...)
in our unique company dining room and impromptu "test kitchen"
known as the **Vera**nda. The energy and creativity this cookbook
represents is a reflection of the unique spirit that is Vera Bradley.
Beautifully illustrated with a "look back" at some of our favorite table settings,
you'll also find little notes and stories about some of our recipes that reveal
the special meaning that each has had in the history of our lives.
In celebration of home, family, and friends, we at Vera Bradley invite you
to sample some of the special dishes we have shared with each other.
We're sure you'll enjoy *Our Favorite Recipes*.

Barbara Bradley Baekgaard and Patricia R. Miller

CONTENTS

GOOD MORNING!

BREADS & BRUNCHES

PAGE 8

TASTEFUL BEGINNINGS

APPETIZERS & BEVERAGES

PAGE 30

IT'S THE LITTLE THINGS

SOUPS, SALADS & SIDES

PAGE 54

Dinner Is Served

Entrées

Page 104

On A Sweet Note

Desserts

Page 156

Contributors   Page 200

Index   Page 202

Order Information   Page 208

GOOD MORNING!
BREADS & BRUNCHES

Scalloped Eggs and Cheese

This is a delicious egg alternative for your family's Sunday breakfast.

1 1/2 tablespoons butter
1 1/2 tablespoons flour
1 cup milk
1 teaspoon Worcestershire sauce
1/4 teaspoon salt
1/8 teaspoon pepper

1/8 teaspoon paprika
1 cup finely crushed bread crumbs
6 hard-cooked eggs, sliced
1/2 cup shredded sharp Cheddar cheese
3 tablespoons butter, melted

Melt 1 1/2 tablespoons butter in a large saucepan. Whisk in the flour to form a paste. Add the milk gradually, whisking constantly. Season with Worcestershire sauce, salt, pepper and paprika. Cook until thickened, whisking constantly.

Layer 1/2 of the bread crumbs, eggs, cheese and the white sauce in a greased baking dish. Sprinkle with the remaining bread crumbs. Drizzle with 3 tablespoons butter. Bake at 350 degrees for 40 minutes or until the sauce is bubbly and the top is light brown.

David Goodman
Vera Bradley Creative Coordinator

*Friday mornings at Vera Bradley are always special . . . and not just on payday! It's our time for a casual "company breakfast." At eight o'clock, an announcement heralds, "Breakfast is ready!" We gather in the cafe-style area known as the **Vera**nda, or some may enjoy a cup of coffee and a bite on the garden patio just outside. Each department takes its turn at making breakfast, and Oh! . . . what a treat! Whether it's fresh fruit and assorted breads or more elaborate affairs like our Cutting Department's hotcakes with maple syrup and sausage, it's always a nice start to the day. Holidays are a great excuse for theme breakfasts, though the green doughnuts for St. Patrick's Day were a little hard to stomach . . .*

Crustless Swiss Quiches

We love these quiches—there is no crust to make.

1/2 cup (1 stick) butter or margarine	1 teaspoon Dijon mustard
1/2 cup flour	9 eggs
1 1/2 cups milk	11 ounces cream cheese, softened
2 1/2 cups cottage cheese	3 cups shredded Swiss cheese
1 teaspoon baking powder	1/3 cup grated Parmesan cheese
1 teaspoon salt	

Melt the butter in a medium saucepan over medium-high heat. Whisk in the flour to form a paste. Add the milk gradually, whisking constantly. Cook until thickened, whisking constantly. Remove from heat. Cool for 15 minutes.

Combine the cottage cheese, baking powder, salt and Dijon mustard in a bowl and mix well. Beat the eggs in a mixing bowl until frothy. Add the cream cheese, cottage cheese mixture and white sauce gradually, beating constantly until smooth. Fold in the Swiss cheese and Parmesan cheese. You may chill, covered, in the refrigerator at this point until ready to bake.

Pour the batter into 2 greased 10-inch pie plates. Bake at 350 degrees for 40 minutes or until puffed and light brown. Cool on a wire rack for 5 minutes. Cut into wedges and serve immediately.

Jill Nichols
Vera Bradley Executive Vice President/COO

Soufflé of Goat Cheese with Smoked Salmon and Dill

YIELD: 4 SERVINGS

1/4 cup (1/2 stick) unsalted butter
1/4 cup flour
1 cup milk
1/2 teaspoon salt
1/2 teaspoon freshly ground pepper

8 ounces fresh soft goat cheese
1/2 cup chopped smoked salmon
1/3 cup finely chopped fresh dillweed
4 eggs, separated

Melt the butter in a saucepan over medium heat until bubbly. Add the flour. Whisk for 30 seconds to form a paste. Add 1/4 cup of the milk, whisking constantly. Reduce heat to low. Add the remaining milk, salt and pepper. Cook for 5 minutes or until thickened, whisking constantly. Stir in the goat cheese. Cook until smooth, stirring constantly. Remove from heat. Stir in the salmon and dillweed. Cool slightly.

Beat the egg yolks in a small bowl until blended. Beat the egg whites in a mixing bowl until stiff peaks form.

Stir the egg yolks into the sauce. Fold the sauce into the stiffly beaten egg whites until no white streaks remain. Do not over stir or the soufflé will deflate. Pour into a greased 1 1/2-quart soufflé dish.

Bake at 300 degrees for 35 to 40 minutes or until golden brown and nearly doubled in size. Serve immediately.

Amy Grinsfelder
Vera Bradley Marketing Design Coordinator

Italian Strata

This is an excellent breakfast strata—especially since it can be made the night before and refrigerated until ready to bake.

1¹/2 pounds mild Italian sausage,
  casings removed
1 pound zucchini, sliced
8 ounces fresh spinach, torn into
  bite-size pieces
1 onion, thinly sliced
1 teaspoon dry mustard
1 teaspoon salt

¹/2 teaspoon freshly ground pepper
2 cups shredded Cheddar cheese
2 cups shredded Swiss cheese
1¹/2 cups milk
7 eggs
10 slices white bread, torn into
  bite-size pieces

Brown the sausage in a skillet, stirring until crumbly. Drain the sausage, reserving the drippings. Sauté the zucchini, spinach and onion in the reserved drippings in the skillet. Combine the sausage, zucchini mixture, dry mustard, salt, pepper, Cheddar cheese, Swiss cheese, milk, eggs and bread in a large bowl and mix well. Chill, covered, in the refrigerator.

Stir the mixture and spoon into a greased 9×13-inch baking dish. Bake at 350 degrees for 1¹/2 hours or until light brown, watching carefully during the last 30 minutes as the strata tends to brown quickly.

Joyce Neubauer
Vera Bradley Classic Steering Committee

Sausage Cheese Strata with Sun-Dried Tomatoes

I first served this at my son's christening. Everyone loved it so much that it has become our first choice for Sunday brunches.

1/2 cup chopped sun-dried tomatoes
12 ounces hot Italian sausage, casings removed
31/2 cups milk
8 eggs
2 teaspoons minced fresh thyme, or 3/4 teaspoon dried thyme
11/2 teaspoons salt

1/4 teaspoon ground pepper
11 slices white bread, cut into 1-inch pieces
1/2 cup chopped onion
1/2 cup freshly grated Parmesan cheese
1 cup grated provolone cheese
1/4 cup crumbled fresh goat cheese
Chopped fresh parsley to taste

Place the sun-dried tomatoes in a small bowl. Add enough hot water to cover. Let stand for 15 minutes or until softened; drain.

Brown the sausage in a medium skillet over medium-high heat, stirring until crumbly. Remove to a bowl lined with paper towels to drain using a slotted spoon.

Whisk the milk, eggs, thyme, salt and pepper in a large bowl until blended. Add the sun-dried tomatoes, sausage, bread, onion and Parmesan cheese and mix well. Spoon into a buttered 9×13-inch baking dish. Chill, covered, for 4 to 12 hours.

Bake, uncovered, at 375 degrees for 45 minutes or until puffed and golden brown. Sprinkle with the provolone cheese and goat cheese. Bake for 10 minutes or until melted. Cool on a wire rack for 5 minutes. Sprinkle with parsley and serve immediately.

Stefanie Chevillet
Vera Bradley Customer Service

Apple Strudel Bars

YIELD: 2½ DOZEN

These are wonderful to take to a friend's for
brunch—everyone will be grateful.

2¾ cups flour
1 teaspoon salt
1 cup plus 2 tablespoons shortening
Milk
1 egg yolk, lightly beaten
1¼ cups crushed Wheaties or
   bran cereal
7 to 8 cups thinly sliced peeled apples

2/3 cup sugar
½ teaspoon cinnamon
¼ teapoon allspice
1 egg white
1 cup confectioners' sugar
½ teaspoon vanilla extract
1 to 2 tablespoons water
3 tablespoons finely chopped pecans

Mix the flour and salt in a bowl. Cut in the shortening until crumbly. Add enough milk to the egg yolk in a glass measure to measure 2/3 cup. Stir into the flour mixture to form a ball. Divide into 2 equal portions. Shape each portion into a flattened circle on a lightly floured surface. Roll 1 portion of the pastry into a 10×15-inch rectangle using a floured rolling pin. Fold into thirds. Place on a 10×15-inch baking pan; unfold to cover bottom of pan. Sprinkle the crushed cereal over the pastry. Combine the apples, sugar, cinnamon and allspice in a bowl and toss to mix well. Arrange over the cereal.

Roll the remaining pastry into a 10×15-inch rectangle. Cut into strips or leave whole. Arrange the strips lattice-fashion over the top or fold the whole pastry into thirds and place over the top. Beat the egg white in a mixing bowl until soft peaks form. Spread over the pastry. Bake at 350 degrees for 55 to 60 minutes or until golden brown. Let stand to cool.

Mix the confectioners' sugar and vanilla in a small bowl. Add enough of the water to make a glaze consistency, stirring constantly. Drizzle over the cooled crust. Sprinkle with the pecans. Cut into 1½×3-inch bars.

Sue Britton
Vera Bradley Marketing Manager

Best-Ever Cinnamon Rolls

Picture it: A warm kitchen in the early morning hours. A pot of fresh coffee is brewing. The day has not quite begun for the rest of the world, but I can see my black Lab, Julius, helping himself to the hot cinnamon rolls on the kitchen table.

4 to 4 1/2 cups flour	2 egg yolks
1 envelope fast-rising dry yeast	1/4 cup (1/2 stick) butter or margarine,
2/3 cup each milk and water	softened
1/2 cup sugar	1/3 cup sugar
1/2 cup vegetable oil	4 teaspoons cinnamon
1/2 teaspoon salt	Cream Cheese Frosting (below)

Mix 2 cups of the flour and yeast in a large mixing bowl. Combine the milk, water, 1/2 cup sugar, oil and salt in a small saucepan. Heat over medium heat until warm, stirring frequently. Add the milk mixture and egg yolks to the flour mixture. Beat at medium speed for 30 seconds. Increase the speed to high and beat for 3 minutes. Stir in as much of the remaining flour as possible using a wooden spoon.

Knead in enough of the remaining flour on a lightly floured surface to form a soft dough that is smooth and elastic. Let rise, covered, for 10 minutes.

Roll into a 12×14-inch rectangle. Spread with the butter. Sprinkle with a mixture of 1/3 cup sugar and cinnamon. Roll as for a jelly roll, beginning at the long end. Press the seam to seal. Cut into 12 slices. Place in a greased 9×13-inch baking pan. Let rise, covered, in a warm draft-free place for 20 minutes or until doubled in bulk.

Bake at 375 degrees for 20 minutes or until golden brown. Cool slightly before removing from the pan. Frost with Cream Cheese Frosting. Serve warm.

Cream Cheese Frosting

3 ounces cream cheese, softened	1/2 teaspoon vanilla extract
3 tablespoons butter or margarine,	1 tablespoon milk
softened	1 1/2 cups confectioners' sugar

Beat the cream cheese, butter and vanilla in a mixing bowl until light and fluffy. Add the milk and beat well. Add the confectioners' sugar gradually, beating constantly at high speed until smooth. Do not use reduced-fat cream cheese in this recipe.

Amy Grinsfelder
Vera Bradley Marketing Design Coordinator

Blueberry Muffins Supreme

YIELD: 1 DOZEN

My friend Denise and I went blueberry picking and the bushes were full of berries. We quickly filled all the containers we had brought. She went back to the car in search of more vessels for our precious cargo, while I continued picking. Well, I filled everything in sight, including my shirttails! I was prepared to eat my way out of the patch, if necessary, but Denise eventually came to my rescue.

$1/2$ cup rolled oats
$1 1/2$ cups flour
$1 1/4$ teaspoons baking powder
$1/2$ teaspoon salt
$1/4$ teaspoon baking soda
$1/2$ cup sugar

$1/2$ cup orange juice
$1/2$ cup vegetable oil
1 cup blueberries
2 tablespoons sugar
$1/2$ teaspoon cinnamon

Combine the oats, flour, baking powder, salt, baking soda, $1/2$ cup sugar, orange juice and oil in a large bowl and mix well. Fold in the blueberries. Spoon into muffin cups lined with paper liners. Mix 2 tablespoons sugar and cinnamon in a small bowl. Sprinkle over the batter. Bake at 400 degrees for 18 to 20 minutes or until golden brown.

Becky Bennett
Vera Bradley Product Development Team

Danish Puffs

This recipe appears to be a "fancy" pastry that takes expertise to create, but it really only requires three simple steps. It's a classy breakfast treat or coffee accompaniment. If you love the taste of almonds, you'll love this coffee cake!

1/2 cup (1 stick) butter	1 teaspoon almond extract
1 cup flour	1 cup flour
2 tablespoons water	3 eggs
1/2 cup (1 stick) butter	Confectioners' Sugar Glaze (below)
1 cup water	Slivered almonds

Cut 1/2 cup butter into 1 cup flour in a bowl until crumbly. Sprinkle with 2 tablespoons water. Mix with a fork to form a ball. Divide into 2 equal portions. Pat each portion into a 12×13-inch rectangle on an ungreased baking sheet, placing about 3 inches apart.

Bring 1/2 cup butter and 1 cup water to a boil in a medium saucepan. Remove from heat. Add the almond flavoring and 1 cup flour immediately. Cook over low heat for about 1 minute or until the mixture forms a ball, stirring constantly. Remove from heat. Add the eggs. Beat until smooth and glossy. Spread over each rectangle. Bake at 350 degrees for 1 hour or until the topping is crisp and brown. Let stand until cool. Topping will shrink and fall, forming a custard top. Spread with Confectioners' Sugar Glaze. Sprinkle with almonds.

Confectioners' Sugar Glaze

1 1/2 cups confectioners' sugar	1 1/2 teaspoons vanilla extract
2 tablespoons butter, softened	1 to 2 tablespoons warm water

Combine the confectioners' sugar, butter and vanilla in a mixing bowl and beat until smooth. Add the warm water 1 teaspoon at a time, beating constantly until thick enough to drizzle.

Sue Britton
Vera Bradley Marketing Manager

Delicious Coffee Cake

YIELD: 15 SERVINGS

1 cup chopped pecans
1 cup packed brown sugar
1 teaspoon cinnamon
1 (2-layer) package yellow cake mix
1 (4-ounce) package vanilla instant
   pudding mix

1 (4-ounce) package butterscotch
   instant pudding mix
4 eggs
1/2 cup vegetable oil
1 cup water
1 teaspoon vanilla extract

Mix the pecans, brown sugar and cinnamon in a bowl. Combine the cake mix, pudding mixes, eggs, oil, water and vanilla in a large mixing bowl and beat until smooth. Pour 1/2 of the batter into a greased 9×13-inch baking pan. Sprinkle with 1/2 of the pecan mixture. Pour the remaining batter over the layers. Sprinkle with the remaining pecan mixture. Bake at 325 degrees for 20 to 30 minutes or until golden brown. Serve plain or topped with whipped cream.

Jennifer Kennedy
Friend of Vera Bradley Designs

Sunday-Best Coffee Cake

YIELD: 16 SERVINGS

Our recipe testers found this recipe *so* good—it was tested by all of them.

1 cup walnuts or pecans, chopped
5 tablespoons brown sugar
1 teaspoon cinnamon
1/2 teaspoon pumpkin pie spice
1 cup (2 sticks) butter or margarine,
   softened
2 cups sugar

3 eggs
1 cup sour cream
1 teaspoon vanilla extract
2 cups flour
1 teaspoon baking powder
1/4 teaspoon salt
Confectioners' sugar

Mix the walnuts, brown sugar, cinnamon and pumpkin pie spice in a small bowl. Beat the butter, sugar and eggs in a mixing bowl until light and fluffy. Beat in the sour cream and vanilla. Fold in the flour, baking powder and salt. Spoon 1/2 of the batter into a greased and floured tube pan. Cover with the walnut mixture, making sure the mixture does not touch the side of the pan. Spoon the remaining batter over the top. Bake at 350 degrees for 1 hour or until a tester inserted in the center comes out clean. Let stand until almost cool. Invert onto a serving plate. Sprinkle with confectioners' sugar.

Joan Bradley Reedy
Vera Bradley Sales Representative
Daughter of Vera Bradley

Raspberry Cream Cheese Coffee Cake

This has quickly become a favorite of all at Vera Bradley.

2 1/4 cups flour
3/4 cup sugar
3/4 cup butter or margarine
1/2 teaspoon baking powder
1/2 teaspoon baking soda
1/4 teaspoon salt
3/4 cup sour cream

1 egg
1 teaspoon almond extract
8 ounces cream cheese, softened
1/4 cup sugar
1 egg
1/2 cup raspberry preserves
1/2 cup slivered almonds

Combine the flour and 3/4 cup sugar in a large bowl. Cut in the butter until crumbly. Reserve 1 cup of the crumb mixture. Add the baking powder, baking soda, salt, sour cream, 1 egg and almond flavoring to the remaining crumb mixture and mix well. Spread over the bottom and 2 1/2 inches up the side of a greased and floured 9- or 10-inch springform pan.

Combine the cream cheese, 1/4 cup sugar and 1 egg in a mixing bowl and beat until smooth. Pour into the prepared pan. Spoon the preserves over the cream cheese layer.

Mix the reserved crumb mixture and almonds in a bowl. Sprinkle over the top. Bake at 350 degrees for 45 to 55 minutes or until the filling is set and the crust is a deep golden brown. Cool for 15 minutes. Remove the side of the pan. Serve warm or cool. Refrigerate any leftovers.

Debbie Wilson
Vera Bradley Executive Administrative Assistant

Crispy Waffles

YIELD: 4 SERVINGS

Crispy and delicious, these are truly the BEST waffles ever! If you don't own a
waffle iron . . . *this is the reason to buy one!*

2 cups baking mix   1 1/3 cups club soda
1 egg   1/2 cup vegetable oil

Combine the baking mix, egg, club soda and oil in a bowl and beat with a wire
whisk until smooth. Pour as needed into a preheated waffle iron. Bake until
golden brown. Serve with your favorite toppings.

Barbara Bradley Baekgaard
President and Co-Founder of Vera Bradley

Traditional Banana Bread with Pecans

YIELD: 12 SERVINGS

Sometimes, you just can't improve an old standby. I've tried several banana
breads, but this is still a favorite with friends and family.

2 very ripe medium bananas, cut into   2 eggs
   1-inch pieces   1/4 cup milk
1/2 cup (1 stick) butter, cut into   2 teaspoons lemon juice
   6 pieces   1 teaspoon baking soda
1 1/2 cups flour   1/2 teaspoon salt
3/4 cup sugar   1/2 cup pecans, chopped

Process the bananas and butter in a food processor until blended. Add the
flour, sugar, eggs, milk, lemon juice, baking soda and salt. Process for 20
seconds. Scrape the side of the bowl and fold in the pecans. Spoon into a
greased 5×9-inch loaf pan. Bake at 350 degrees for 55 to 60 minutes or until
the loaf springs back when lightly touched in the center. Cool on a wire rack
for 10 minutes before serving.

Stacie Gray
Vera Bradley Customer Service

Lemon Blueberry Bread

This recipe was given to me by a very good friend when our family was stationed in Rome, New York. My family loves blueberries, and this is a really delicious way to have them year-round. (You can use fresh or frozen blueberries.)

1 1/2 cups flour	2 eggs
1 teaspoon baking powder	1/2 cup milk
1/8 teaspoon salt	2 teaspoons lemon zest
6 tablespoons butter or margarine, softened	1 cup blueberries
	2 teaspoons flour
1 cup sugar	Lemon Glaze (below)

Mix 1 1/2 cups flour, baking powder and salt together. Cream the butter and sugar in a mixing bowl until light and fluffy. Beat in the eggs 1 at a time. Add the flour mixture alternately with the milk, beating well after each addition and beginning and ending with the flour mixture. Stir in the lemon zest. Toss the blueberries with 2 teaspoons flour in a bowl until coated. Fold into the batter. Pour into a greased 5x9-inch loaf pan.

Bake at 350 degrees for 55 to 60 minutes or until the loaf tests done. Pierce the warm bread with a fork. Pour Lemon Glaze over the top. Cool in the pan for 30 minutes or longer. Remove to a wire rack to cool completely.

Lemon Glaze

1/3 cup sugar	3 tablespoons lemon juice

Combine the sugar and lemon juice in a small saucepan. Heat until the sugar dissolves, stirring frequently.

Becky Bennett
Vera Bradley Product Development Team

Pumpkin Tea Bread

YIELD: 2 LOAVES

It's not just another pumpkin bread recipe . . . this one
will take the blue ribbon.

2 1/2 cups all-purpose flour
1 cup whole wheat flour
2 teaspoons baking soda
1/2 teaspoon baking powder
1 1/2 teaspoons salt
1 teaspoon cinnamon
2/3 cup shortening

2 2/3 cups sugar
4 eggs
2 cups canned or mashed cooked
    pumpkin
2/3 cup water
1 cup pecans, chopped
1 cup raisins

Sift the all-purpose flour, whole wheat flour, baking soda, baking powder, salt
and cinnamon together.

Cream the shortening and sugar in a mixing bowl until light and fluffy.
Add the eggs 1 at a time, beating well after each addition. Add the pumpkin
and water and beat well. Stir in the flour mixture using a wooden spoon until
blended. Fold in the pecans and raisins.

Pour into 2 greased and floured 5×9-inch loaf pans. Bake at 350 degrees
for 1 hour or until a tester inserted in the center of the loaves comes out clean.
Cool in the pans for 10 minutes. Invert onto a wire rack to cool completely.

Bonnie Stewart Mickelson
Friend of Vera Bradley Designs

Zucchini Bread

YIELD: 2 LOAVES

Our summertime garden was so full of zucchini that we used it in every recipe.
Some recipes we did not try again, but this one was a keeper.

3 cups flour
2 teaspoons baking soda
1/2 teaspoon baking powder
1 teaspoon salt
1 teaspoon cinnamon
3 eggs

1 cup vegetable oil
1 cup sugar
1 cup packed brown sugar
2 cups coarsely shredded zucchini
1 cup pecans, chopped

Sift the flour, baking soda, baking powder, salt and cinnamon together.

Beat the eggs, oil, sugar and brown sugar in a mixing bowl until thick and foamy. Stir in the zucchini. Fold in the flour mixture. Stir in the pecans. Pour into 2 greased and floured 5×9-inch loaf pans. Bake at 350 degrees for 1 hour. Cool for 10 minutes in the pans on a wire rack. Invert onto serving plates. Serve warm.

Palma Ashley
Vera Bradley New Accounts Coordinator

Irish Soda Bread

YIELD: 3 LOAVES

This bread is perfect as a toasted breakfast bread or served
with a bowl of soup for dunking.

6 cups flour
1¹/2 cups sugar
2 teaspoons baking powder
1 teaspoon baking soda
4 or 5 eggs
1 cup buttermilk

1 cup sour cream
1 cup (2 sticks) butter, softened
1 cup golden raisins
1 cup raisins
¹/4 cup caraway seeds (optional)

Sift the flour, sugar, baking powder and baking soda together.
    Beat the eggs in a mixing bowl. Add the buttermilk and sour cream and
blend well. Beat in the butter. Add the flour mixture and beat until smooth.
Stir in the raisins and caraway seeds. Spoon into 3 nonstick 5×9-inch loaf pans.
Bake at 350 degrees for 1 hour.

Misericordia Gift Shop
Chicago, Illinois

Boston Brown Bread

YIELD: 2 LOAVES

1 cup yellow cornmeal
1 cup whole wheat flour
1 cup whole grain rye flour
2 teaspoons baking soda

1 teaspoon salt
2 cups buttermilk
1 cup dark molasses
1 cup dried currants

Butter 2 clean 28-ounce food cans. Mix the cornmeal, whole wheat flour, rye flour, baking soda and salt in a large mixing bowl. Combine the buttermilk, molasses and currants in a medium bowl and whisk well. Add to the flour mixture and blend well. Pour into the prepared cans. Butter 2 pieces of foil large enough to cover the top of each can, overlapping by 2 inches. Place buttered side down over the top of each can and secure with kitchen string.

Place the cans in a large wide stockpot. Pour enough water into the stockpot to come halfway up the sides of the cans. Bring to a boil and reduce the heat to low. Simmer, tightly covered, for about 3 hours or until a tester inserted in the center of each comes out clean, adding additional water as needed to keep the water halfway up the sides.

Remove the cans from the stockpot. Cool in the cans for 15 minutes. Shake gently to remove the bread from the cans.

You may make the bread 1 day in advance. Cool the bread completely and return to the cans. Wrap tightly with foil and store at room temperature. Before serving, place the bread in the covered cans on a wire rack set over simmering water in a large stockpot. Steam for 15 minutes or until heated through.

Denise Mitchell
Vera Bradley Administrative Assistant

Boston Brown Bread is a hearty, heavy bread. Perfect to serve with coffee or tea. You may substitute raisins for the currants if you like. Here's a wonderful Christmas gift idea: Add white citron and chopped walnuts for a very tasty mock fruitcake. Bake as directed, remove from cans to cool, then return fruitcake to the cans. After wrapping in foil or plastic wrap, double-wrap the cans in festive holiday paper. Crimp each end and tie wtih curling ribbons, then slit the paper "tails" with scissors and fluff for a beautiful Victorian "party cracker" look.

French Bread with Herb Butter

French Bread with Herb Butter is great with a steak dinner!

2 loaves French bread
3/4 cup butter or margarine, melted
1/2 cup mixed fresh herbs, such as
   parsley, basil or thyme

1 garlic clove, minced
1/8 teaspoon pepper

Cut each loaf into thin slices to but not through the bottom. Mix the melted butter with the herbs, garlic and pepper in a bowl. Brush between the bread slices. Wrap each loaf in foil. Bake at 350 degrees for 7 to 10 minutes or until heated through. Serve immediately.

Barb Erhardt
Vera Bradley Product Development Coordinator

French Bread with Pesto Parmesan Spread

YIELD: 6 SERVINGS

This is the perfect accompaniment to a summer dinner. I just wrap it in foil and throw it on the grill for a couple of minutes.

8 ounces cream cheese, softened
1/4 cup (1/2 stick) butter, softened
1/2 cup chopped fresh basil
2 tablespoons chopped fresh parsley
3 green onions with tops, thinly sliced

1 garlic clove, chopped
1/4 cup freshly grated Parmesan cheese
1 loaf French bread, cut into
   1/4-inch slices
Cayenne pepper to taste

Process the cream cheese and butter in a food processor until smooth. Add the basil, parsley, green onions, garlic and Parmesan cheese and process to blend. Spoon into a small bowl. Chill, covered, in the refrigerator.

Spread the cream cheese mixture on the bread slices. Sprinkle with additional Parmesan cheese. Sprinkle with cayenne pepper. Place on a baking sheet. Broil until the edges begin to brown. Serve immediately.

Barb Erhardt
Vera Bradley Product Development Coordinator

Out-of-this-World Rolls

YIELD: 2^1/2 DOZEN

The variations on these rolls make them perfect for all occasions.

2 envelopes dry yeast
3/4 cup warm water
2 eggs, beaten
4^1/2 to 5 cups flour
1 cup warm water

^{1}/2 cup shortening
^{1}/2 cup sugar
2 teaspoons salt
Butter or margarine to taste

Dissolve the yeast in ^{3}/4 cup warm water. Let stand for 10 minutes. Combine the yeast mixture, eggs, 2^1/2 cups of the flour, 1 cup warm water, shortening, sugar and salt in a large mixing bowl. Beat at medium speed for 2 minutes or until smooth, scraping the side of the bowl occasionally. Stir in enough of the remaining flour with a wooden spoon to form a soft dough. Let rise, covered, for 1 hour or until doubled in bulk. Punch the dough down. Cover and refrigerate for 8 to 12 hours.

Divide the dough into 2 equal portions. Roll each portion into a rectangle ^{1}/2 inch thick. Spread with butter. Roll as for a jelly roll, starting at the long end. Cut into 1-inch slices. Place open side down in greased muffin cups. Let rise, covered, for 3 hours. Bake at 400 degrees for 12 to 15 minutes or until golden brown.

For Garlic Parmesan Rolls, sprinkle generously with garlic salt and grated Parmesan cheese after spreading with butter. Continue with the basic recipe.

Mercedes Cox
Friend of Vera Bradley Designs

Sesame Holiday Rolls

....

YIELD: 1 DOZEN

We recommend doubling this recipe—no one will eat just one.

1 envelope dry yeast	2 tablespoons olive oil
2 cups flour	1 cup warm water
1 teaspoon salt	1 tablespoon cornmeal
1 teaspoon pepper	1 egg white, lightly beaten
2 teaspoons minced jalapeño chiles	3 tablespoons sesame seeds

Combine the yeast, flour, salt and pepper in a large mixing bowl and mix well. Stir in the chiles. Add the oil and warm water and mix to form a soft dough, adding additional flour if necessary. Knead on a lightly floured surface for 5 minutes or until smooth and elastic. Return to the mixing bowl and cover with a towel. Let rise in a warm draft-free area for 1 hour or until doubled in bulk.

Punch down the dough and return to a lightly floured surface. Knead the dough again. Divide the dough into 12 equal portions, sprinkling with flour as necessary to avoid sticking. Lengthen each portion into a rope 12 inches long. Tie each rope into a knot.

Sprinkle the cornmeal on a nonstick baking sheet. Place each knot on the prepared baking sheet. Let rise for 1 hour or until doubled in bulk. Bake at 350 degrees for 10 minutes. Brush each knot with egg white. Sprinkle with sesame seeds. Bake for 5 to 10 minutes or until golden brown.

Michael Nelaborige
Vera Bradley Marketing Assistant

Tasteful Beginnings
Appetizers & Beverages

Black Bean Hummus

YIELD: 8 SERVINGS

For something a little different, try this southwestern twist on hummus.

2 (15-ounce) cans black beans,
    rinsed, drained
3/4 cup tahini (sesame seed paste)
1/4 cup lemon juice
1/4 cup packed fresh cilantro, chopped
4 green onions, sliced
2 large garlic cloves, minced

2 tablespoons olive oil
1 teaspoon cumin
1/2 teaspoon cayenne pepper
Salt and black pepper to taste
1/2 cup salsa
Pita bread rounds, cut into triangles,
    toasted

Process the black beans, tahini, lemon juice, cilantro, green onions, garlic, oil, cumin and cayenne pepper in a food processor until smooth. Season with salt and black pepper. Spoon into a serving bowl. Top with the salsa. Serve with pita triangles. You may make 1 day in advance and chill, covered, in the refrigerator to enhance the flavor.

Kim Colby
Vera Bradley Vice President of Design

Black Bean Toss

YIELD: 8 SERVINGS

This is the perfect accompaniment to a good margarita on a warm afternoon.

2 (15-ounce) cans black beans,
    rinsed, drained
1 (15-ounce) can diced Mexican
    tomatoes, drained
1 (11-ounce) can whole kernel corn,
    drained
1 (7-ounce) can chopped mild or hot
    green chiles, drained

1/4 to 1/2 cup fresh cilantro, chopped
1/4 cup chopped green onions
1/2 cup salsa
2 tablespoons lime juice
2 tablespoons red wine vinegar
1 1/2 tablespoons olive oil
1/8 teaspoon Tabasco sauce

Combine the black beans, tomatoes, corn, green chiles, cilantro and green onions in a large bowl. Add the salsa, lime juice, vinegar, oil and Tabasco sauce and toss to mix. Chill, covered, for 3 to 10 hours. Serve with blue corn tortilla chips.

Betsy Lewis Harned
Betsy Anne's
Glasgow, Kentucky

Curried Chutney Cheese Ball

YIELD: 8 SERVINGS

I gave this recipe to my sister and my cousin. They both brought it to the *same* party, but everyone devoured the cheese balls! Now, I always double the recipe. (You can freeze the extra one if you don't need both.)

11 ounces cream cheese, softened
1/2 cup chopped green onions
1/2 cup bacon bits
2 teaspoons sour cream

1/2 cup raisins
1/2 teaspoon curry powder
1/2 cup chopped pecans or walnuts
1 jar chutney

Beat the cream cheese in a medium mixing bowl until smooth. Add the green onions, bacon bits, sour cream, raisins, curry powder and pecans and mix well. Shape into a ball. Chill, covered, for 6 hours or longer. Place the cheese ball on a small serving platter. Pour the chutney over the top. Serve at room temperature with crackers or French bread pieces.

Joanie Byrne Hall
Granddaughter of Vera Bradley

Warm Bleu Cheese, Bacon and Garlic Dip

YIELD: 8 SERVINGS

Since this appetizer is always the first one gone,
we recommend doubling the recipe.

7 slices bacon, chopped
2 garlic cloves, minced
8 ounces cream cheese, softened
1/4 cup half-and-half

4 ounces bleu cheese, crumbled
2 tablespoons chopped fresh chives
3 tablespoons smoked almonds,
　chopped

Cook the bacon in a skillet until almost cooked through; drain. Add the garlic. Cook until the bacon is crisp.

Beat the cream cheese in a mixing bowl until smooth. Add the half-and-half and blend well. Stir in the bacon mixture, bleu cheese and chives. Spoon into an ovenproof serving dish and cover with foil. Bake at 350 degrees for 30 minutes or until heated through. Uncover and sprinkle with the almonds. Serve with sliced apples, toasted pita crisps, French bread baguettes or crackers.

Phyllis Loy
Vera Bradley Customer Service

Tomato Pesto Cheese Mold

YIELD: 8 SERVINGS

I serve this every year at our Christmas party. One year I left it off the
hors d'oeuvre list and everyone asked about it.

16 ounces cream cheese, softened   1/2 cup sun-dried tomatoes, drained
1 1/2 cups (3 sticks) butter, softened   1 cup Sunflower Seed Pesto (below)

Process the cream cheese and butter in a food processor until smooth. Spread
1/3 of the cream cheese mixture in a 7-cup mold. Layer the sun-dried tomatoes,
1/2 of the remaining cream cheese mixture, Sunflower Seed Pesto and remaining
cream cheese mixture in the prepared mold. Chill, covered, for 2 to 10 hours.
Unmold onto a serving platter. Serve at room temperature with crackers or
French bread baguettes.

Sunflower Seed Pesto

YIELD: 1 1/2 TO 2 CUPS

4 garlic cloves   1 cup olive oil
3 cups firmly packed fresh basil   1 cup sunflower kernels
1 cup grated Parmesan cheese

Process the garlic in a food processor until finely minced. Add the basil,
Parmesan cheese, oil and sunflower kernels. Process for 1 minute or until
smooth. Spoon into a small bowl. Chill, covered, in the refrigerator.

Leslie K. Byrne
Daughter-in-law of Barbara Bradley Baekgaard

Beer Cheese Dip

YIELD: 8 SERVINGS

These are a few of our favorite things!

3 ounces cream cheese, softened
8 ounces sharp Cheddar cheese,
  shredded
1 garlic clove, minced

1 tablespoon Worcestershire sauce
1/2 teaspoon dry mustard
1/4 teaspoon cayenne pepper
1/4 cup beer

Beat the cream cheese and Cheddar cheese at medium speed in a mixing bowl until combined. Add the garlic, Worcestershire sauce, dry mustard and cayenne pepper and beat well. Add the beer gradually, beating constantly. Spoon into a serving bowl. Chill, covered, for 1 hour. Serve with crusty bread or crackers.

Katie Burns
Friend of Vera Bradley Designs

White Mexican Cheese Dip

YIELD: 8 SERVINGS

This is so easy it can barely be called a recipe, but every time
I make it someone wants the "recipe."

2 cups sour cream
16 ounces cottage cheese
8 ounces pepper-Jack cheese, grated

1 bunch green onions, sliced
1/2 jalapeño chile, minced, or Tabasco
  sauce to taste

Combine the sour cream, cottage cheese, pepper-Jack cheese and green onions in a bowl and mix well. Add the jalapeño chile and mix well. Serve with tortilla chips or corn chips.

Amy Ray
Granddaughter of Vera Bradley

Warm Swiss Cheese and Bacon Dip

8 ounces cream cheese, softened
1 cup grated Swiss cheese
1/2 cup mayonnaise

2 tablespoons chopped green onions
1/2 cup bacon bits
1/2 cup butter cracker crumbs

Combine the cream cheese, Swiss cheese, mayonnaise and green onions in a bowl and mix well. Spoon into a baking dish. Bake at 350 degrees for 20 minutes. Sprinkle with the bacon bits and cracker crumbs. Serve warm with crackers. You may substitute 1/2 cup sliced almonds for the butter cracker crumbs for a different twist.

Nancy Graham
Vera Bradley Customer Service—Retired

Roasted Red Pepper Dip

Nancy Graham was hosting one of our famous Customer Service get-togethers and I volunteered to make this. It was so good that *everyone* there wanted the recipe. Very tasty!!!

2 red bell peppers
1 (4-ounce) jar oil-pack sun-dried
   tomatoes
2 garlic cloves
2 teaspoons cumin
1/4 cup chopped fresh cilantro

1 to 2 pickled jalapeño chiles, coarsely
   chopped
White part only of 1 bunch green
   onions, chopped
6 ounces cream cheese, softened
1/2 teaspoon salt

Cut the bell peppers into halves and discard the seeds. Place cut side down on a baking sheet. Broil until the tops are black. Place in a nonrecycled brown paper bag or a sealable plastic food storage bag. Let stand for 10 to 15 minutes. Remove the skin from the bell peppers. Cool and press between paper towels to remove excess moisture.

Drain the tomatoes and pat dry. Process the roasted bell peppers, tomatoes, garlic, cumin, cilantro, chiles, green onions, cream cheese and salt in a food processor until smooth. Adjust the seasonings, adding additional jalapeño chiles if desired. Serve with blue corn chips.

You may use one 4-ounce jar roasted red peppers instead of roasting your own peppers.

Phyllis Loy
Vera Bradley Customer Service

Crowd-Pleasing Taco Dip

YIELD: 15 SERVINGS

The name says it all!

2 cups sour cream
16 ounces cream cheese, softened
2 (8-ounce) jars picante sauce or salsa
2 pounds ground beef
2 envelopes taco seasoning mix

16 ounces sharp Cheddar cheese,
  shredded
2 cups chopped lettuce
1 cup chopped tomatoes

Beat the sour cream and cream cheese in a mixing bowl until smooth. Spread in a 9×13-inch dish. Pour the picante sauce over the cream cheese mixture.

Brown the ground beef in a skillet, stirring until crumbly; drain. Stir in the taco seasoning mix. Layer over the picante sauce. Continue layering with the cheese, lettuce and tomatoes. Serve at room temperature with tortilla chips.

LeAnn Frankle
Vera Bradley Accounting Team

Sombrero Spread

YIELD: 8 SERVINGS

This Mexican dip has been *the* favorite at our house for over twenty years. When you take this to a carry-in, take the recipe along . . . everyone will want it!

1 pound ground beef
1/2 cup chopped onion
1 (16-ounce) jar taco sauce
1 (16-ounce) can kidney beans
1/4 cup chili sauce

1/4 cup ketchup
1 teaspoon red pepper
Salt to taste
Shredded Cheddar cheese

Brown the ground beef with the onion in a skillet, stirring until the ground beef is crumbly; drain. Add the taco sauce, undrained kidney beans, chili sauce, ketchup, red pepper and salt and mix well. Simmer for 30 minutes or longer. Spoon into a serving dish. Sprinkle with cheese. Serve with tortilla chips.

Becky Bennett
Vera Bradley Product Development Team

Millie's Curried Dip

YIELD: 4 TO 6 SERVINGS

This dip does not have to be prepared ahead of time, but if you do
it will intensify the flavors. You'll love it as a dip for all sorts
of pretty things from the garden.

1 cup mayonnaise
2 tablespoons Durkee's seasoning
1 tablespoon (rounded) prepared
   horseradish
1/2 small garlic clove, minced

1 teaspoon celery seeds
1 teaspoon curry powder
1 teaspoon seasoned salt
1/2 teaspoon Worcestershire sauce
1/8 teaspoon Tabasco sauce

Combine the mayonnaise, Durkee's seasoning, horseradish, garlic, celery seeds,
curry powder, seasoned salt, Worcestershire sauce and Tabasco sauce in a bowl
and mix well. Chill, covered, in the refrigerator. Serve with fresh vegetables,
such as carrot and celery sticks, cucumber and bell pepper slices, cherry
tomatoes and green onions.

Bonnie Stewart Mickelson
Friend of Vera Bradley Designs

Clam Dip

8 ounces cream cheese, softened
1 garlic clove, minced
2 teaspoons lemon juice
1 1/2 teaspoons Worcestershire sauce
1/2 teaspoon salt

1/2 teaspoon pepper
1 (7-ounce) can minced clams, drained
1/4 cup clam juice

Combine the cream cheese, garlic, lemon juice, Worcestershire sauce, salt and pepper in a bowl and blend well. Stir in the clams and clam juice. Chill, covered, in the refrigerator. Spoon into a serving bowl. Serve with large scoop corn chips.

Susie Bruce
Vera Bradley Merchandising Coordinator—Retired

The Ultimate Crab Dip

6 ounces cream cheese, softened
3/4 cup mayonnaise
8 ounces Swiss cheese, grated
1 package Snow Flake crab meat, thawed, drained

1 onion, minced
1 hard-cooked egg, chopped
1/4 teaspoon dry mustard
1/2 teaspoon paprika
Ground pepper to taste

Beat the cream cheese and mayonnaise in a mixing bowl until smooth. Add the Swiss cheese, crab meat, onion, egg, dry mustard, paprika and pepper and beat well. Serve with crackers.

You may heat the dip in a chafing dish and serve hot or spread on toasted pumpernickel bread for an open-faced sandwich. Add chopped celery and green bell pepper for a salad or add rice or noodles for an entrée.

Lou Alexander
Legend Lake Golf Club
Chardon, Ohio

Smoked Salmon Dip

YIELD: 4 SERVINGS

Guests will be "swimming upstream" in your buffet line
for this tantalizing appetizer!

4 ounces smoked salmon, shredded
1/3 cup heavy cream
1/2 teaspoon capers, drained

1/8 teaspoon freshly ground pepper
Tabasco sauce to taste
Freshly ground pepper to taste

Process the salmon, cream, capers, 1/8 teaspoon pepper and Tabasco sauce in a food processor until smooth. Spoon into a serving dish. Sprinkle with pepper to taste. Chill, covered, for 6 hours or longer. Serve with toast points or crackers.

Phyllis Loy
Vera Bradley Customer Service

Smoked White Fish Pâté

YIELD: 8 SERVINGS

Use smoked white fish from Northern Michigan for the best results.
If you can't get there, your local grocer's selection will work.

1 1/2 pounds smoked white fish, finely
   chopped
1/2 cup finely chopped red onion
1/2 cup snipped fresh chives
2 tablespoons plus 2 teaspoons capers,
   drained, coarsely chopped

2 tablespoons plus 2 teaspoons Dijon
   mustard
Cracked white pepper to taste
2 cucumbers, thinly sliced

Combine the fish, onion, chives, capers and Dijon mustard in a bowl. Season with white pepper. Stir with a fork until the mixture is thoroughly combined. Divide into 2 portions. Shape each portion into thick patties. Wrap each tightly in plastic wrap. Chill in the refrigerator for 24 hours.

Place the cucumber slices in concentric circles in the middle of 2 serving platters. Unwrap the patties and place in the center of each cucumber bed. Serve with crackers or toast points.

Lyn Killoran
Friend of Vera Bradley

Kathleen's Marinated Shrimp

YIELD: 4 SERVINGS

This has been one of our family favorites for years. I finally asked my mom who Kathleen was. It turns out it's her friend Taff Silliman, who I'd never known as "Kathleen." A good story for a great dish—pretty too.

2¹/₂ cups large shrimp, peeled,
   deveined, cooked
2 cups red onion rings
7 or 8 bay leaves
1¹/₂ cups olive oil

³/₄ cup white vinegar
2¹/₂ tablespoons capers, drained
2¹/₂ teaspoons celery salt
1¹/₂ teaspoons salt
¹/₈ teaspoon Tabasco sauce

Alternate layers of the shrimp, onion rings and bay leaves in a large clear serving bowl. Combine the oil, vinegar, capers, celery salt, salt and Tabasco sauce in a bowl and blend well. Pour over the layers. Marinate, covered, in the refrigerator for 24 hours. Serve the shrimp with cocktail sauce if desired.

Stefanie Chevillet
Vera Bradley Customer Service

Baked Brie with
Caramelized Onions and Tomato Preserves

YIELD: 8 SERVINGS

A party starter with flair!

2 teaspoons butter or margarine
1 small onion, cut into thin wedges
¹/₃ cup tomato preserves or mango
   chutney

¹/₂ teaspoon snipped fresh rosemary
¹/₈ teaspoon crushed red pepper flakes
1 (8-ounce) wheel Brie cheese

Melt the butter in a small saucepan. Add the onion. Cook, covered, over low heat for 15 minutes, stirring occasionally. Combine the preserves, rosemary and red pepper flakes in a small bowl and mix well.

Cut a very thin slice from the top of the cheese and discard. Place the cheese in the center of an ungreased 9-inch pie plate. Top with the preserve mixture and sautéed onion. Bake at 325 degrees for 10 to 12 minutes or until the cheese is softened and warm, but not runny. Serve with crackers or French bread baguettes.

Kim Colby
Vera Bradley Vice President of Design

Chili Brie in Sourdough

I used to get together with several of my good friends on Monday nights to watch our favorite nighttime soap opera, *Melrose Place*. Each of us would bring a favorite treat, and it was always a challenge to bring the best one (and anyone caught bringing the same one again was chastised for their *rerun*). This one was an instant hit, and was gone before the first "cat fight!"

1 teaspoon chili powder
1/2 teaspoon dry mustard
1/2 teaspoon garlic powder
1/2 teaspoon sugar

1 (1-pound) round loaf sourdough
　bread
1 tablespoon butter, softened
1 (8-ounce) wheel Brie cheese

Combine the chili powder, dry mustard, garlic powder and sugar in a bowl and mix well. Cut a circle from the top of the bread slightly larger than the diameter of the cheese; reserve the bread top. Remove the center of the bread to form a shell and reserve.

Spread the butter in the bread shell. Sprinkle with 2 teaspoons of the spice mixture. Make 2-inch cuts around the edge at 1-inch intervals. Remove and discard the rind from the cheese. Place in the bread shell. Sprinkle the cheese with the remaining spice mixture. Replace the top of the bread. Place on a baking sheet. Bake at 350 degrees for 20 to 30 minutes or until golden brown.

To serve, remove the bread top and tear into bite-size pieces. Tear the reserved center into bite-size pieces. Dip the bread pieces into the hot cheese. You may also serve with crackers.

Kathy Reedy Ray
Vera Bradley Marketing Associate
Granddaughter of Vera Bradley

Baked Chèvre with Sun-Dried Tomatoes and Basil

YIELD: 8 SERVINGS

Different, easy and delicious!

4 ounces sun-dried tomatoes
1 cup boiling water
1/2 cup minced fresh basil
1/2 teaspoon minced garlic

8 ounces chèvre or other fine goat
   cheese
Olive oil for coating

Place the tomatoes in boiling water in a saucepan. Let stand for 15 to 20 minutes or until softened; drain and mince. Combine with the basil and garlic in a bowl and mix well.

    Place the cheese in a small ovenproof serving dish coated with olive oil. Bake at 400 degrees for 15 minutes or until melted. Spoon the tomato mixture over the top. Serve with crackers.

Kim Colby
Vera Bradley Vice President of Design

Caviar Pie

YIELD: 8 SERVINGS

This recipe comes from Glenna's mother, Roberta May "Boots" Yott. It has been one of Glenna's family favorites for years. She was kind enough to share such a unique, delicious recipe with us.

5 hard-cooked eggs, finely chopped
1/2 cup (1 stick) butter, softened
1 small white onion, finely chopped

2 (4-ounce) jars caviar
1 cup sour cream

Combine the eggs and butter in a small mixing bowl and mix well to form a paste. Spread on an 8-inch round platter with side. Chill, covered, for 1 hour.

    Layer the onion and caviar over the egg mixture. Spread the sour cream evenly over the top. Serve with water crackers and vodka.

Glenna Reno
Vera Bradley Sales Representative

Artichoke Phyllo Flowers

YIELD: 2 1/2 DOZEN

1/4 cup (1/2 stick) butter
1 bunch green onions, sliced
2 garlic cloves, minced
1 (14-ounce) can artichoke hearts,
   drained, finely chopped
8 ounces ricotta cheese

1 egg, lightly beaten
1/2 cup milk
1/2 cup grated Parmesan cheese
2 tablespoons snipped chives
Salt and pepper to taste
9 sheets frozen phyllo, thawed

Melt the butter in a medium skillet over medium heat. Add the green onions and garlic. Sauté for 2 minutes. Add the artichoke hearts. Sauté for 5 to 6 minutes or until brown. Remove from heat.

Combine the ricotta cheese and egg in a medium mixing bowl and mix well. Add the milk and blend well. Stir in the Parmesan cheese and chives. Fold in the artichoke mixture. Season with salt and pepper.

Unroll the phyllo and cover with waxed paper and a damp towel. Lay 1 sheet of phyllo on a flat work surface and spray with nonstick cooking spray. Repeat 2 more times, forming a 3-layer stack. Cut into 5 strips lengthwise and 4 strips horizontally, forming 20 squares. Place 1 square at an angle over a miniature muffin cup; place another square at the opposite angle. Press into the muffin cup. Repeat the process until all the cups are filled with 2 phyllo squares.

Spoon the artichoke filling evenly into the phyllo cups. Bake at 350 degrees for 15 to 20 minutes or until the filling is set and the phyllo is golden brown. Cool for 5 minutes. Remove from the cups with the tip of a knife. You may make these ahead, freeze and reheat just before serving.

Amy Grinsfelder
Vera Bradley Marketing Design Coordinator

Whether it's delicate hors d'oeuvre or a formal dinner, we've always believed that "presentation is everything." Our golf and tennis event, the Vera Bradley Classic, raises money for the Vera Bradley Foundation for Breast Cancer. It includes several large dinner parties, entertaining nearly 1,000 sponsors, participants, and special guests. In Vera Bradley style, the largest tent in the state is raised.

Return to Happiness fabric, fresh flowers, elegant table settings, and delectable food bring the tent to life. Though you may not entertain on this scale, any dinner can feel like an event if you spare no expense in hospitality, and serve the simplest foods with a flair for presentation.

Appetizer Steak Kabobs

YIELD: 10 TO 12 SERVINGS

These are a deliciously different change from the usual fare.

2 pounds sirloin steak, cut into
  bite-size pieces
2 cups mushrooms, stems removed
1 medium onion, cut into wedges
1 green or red bell pepper, cut into
  bite-size pieces

$^1/_2$ cup vegetable oil
$^1/_2$ cup Worcestershire sauce
1 cup soy sauce

Arrange the steak, mushrooms, onion and bell pepper in a shallow dish. Blend the oil, Worcestershire sauce and soy sauce in a bowl. Pour over the steak mixture. Marinate, covered, in the refrigerator for 2 days.

Drain the steak mixture, discarding the marinade. Skewer 1 piece of steak, 1 mushroom, 1 onion wedge and 1 bell pepper piece onto a white wooden pick. Repeat until all of the ingredients are used. Place on a baking sheet. Broil for a few minutes or until the steak is done to taste, turning occasionally and watching carefully. You may make these kabobs ahead of time and serve at room temperature.

Pat Kramer
Letter Perfect at the Balcony
Schenectady, New York

Vickki's Hors d'Oeuvre

YIELD: 8 SERVINGS

Here's a quick appetizer to whip up that's always a crowd-pleaser.

$^1/_2$ onion, chopped
1 (6-ounce) can chopped black olives,
  drained
$^1/_2$ cup mayonnaise

1 teaspoon curry powder
8 ounces shredded white Cheddar
  cheese
English muffin halves

Combine the onion, olives, mayonnaise and curry powder in a bowl and mix well. Stir in the cheese. Spread on English muffin halves. Place on a baking sheet. Broil until the tops are brown. Cut into quarters and serve.

Joanie Byrne Hall
Granddaughter of Vera Bradley

Mediterranean Pizza

This is great served as an appetizer or as a wonderful vegetarian entrée.

Cornmeal
1 (8-count) can crescent rolls
2 tablespoons olive oil
³/4 teaspoon garlic powder
1 (15-ounce) can chick-peas, drained
¹/2 (4-ounce) jar roasted red peppers, drained
1 garlic clove, minced

1 tablespoon lemon juice
1¹/2 cups chopped seeded Italian tomatoes
1 (14-ounce) can artichoke hearts, drained, chopped
1 (4-ounce) can sliced black olives, drained
1 cup crumbled feta cheese

Sprinkle cornmeal over a pizza stone or spray a baking sheet with nonstick cooking spray and sprinkle with cornmeal. Unroll the crescent roll dough, pressing the perforations to seal. Brush with the oil. Sprinkle with the garlic powder. Place on the prepared pizza stone or baking sheet. Bake at 425 degrees for 3 to 5 minutes or until light brown.

Process the chick-peas, roasted peppers, garlic and lemon juice in a food processor or blender for 2 minutes or until smooth. Spread over the crust. Top with the tomatoes, artichoke hearts, olives and cheese. Bake for 10 to 12 minutes or until the edges are golden brown. Cut into appetizer-size portions.

Emilie Robertson
Vera Bradley Customer Service

Red Pepper and Goat Cheese Pizza

YIELD: 8 SERVINGS

Cut into 1-inch pieces and serve as an appetizer, or
serve with a lettuce salad as an entrée.

10 sun-dried tomatoes
4 ounces goat cheese, softened
3 ounces cream cheese, softened
1 baked homemade pizza crust or
  purchased pizza crust, such as
  Boboli
2 teaspoons oregano
2 teaspoons basil
2 teaspoons Italian seasoning

1 cup trimmed fresh spinach
1 (4-ounce) jar roasted red peppers,
  rinsed, chopped
1 (14-ounce) can artichoke hearts,
  drained, chopped
3/4 cup grated Parmesan or Romano
  cheese
1 cup crumbled feta cheese

Soak the sun-dried tomatoes in hot water to cover in a bowl until softened;
drain and pat dry. If the tomatoes are packed in oil, you don't need to soak them.

Beat the goat cheese and cream cheese in a small mixing bowl until
smooth. Spread over the pizza crust. Sprinkle with the oregano, basil and
Italian seasoning. Layer the spinach, roasted peppers, sun-dried tomatoes and
artichoke hearts over the crust. Sprinkle the Parmesan cheese and feta cheese
over the top.

Place on a pizza stone or round baking sheet. Bake at 425 degrees for
15 to 20 minutes or until heated through and the bottom is crisp.

Stefanie Chevillet
Vera Bradley Customer Service

Frog Mix

YIELD: 10 SERVINGS

This recipe is from my favorite little bar in South Carolina. It's a British pub called The Frog & Brassiere. This snack mix recipe came from the owner.

1 bottle Orville Redenbacher's
   butter-flavor popcorn oil
1 envelope ranch salad dressing mix
1 (6-ounce) package Bugles
1 (10-ounce) package Cheez-It
   crackers

1 (12-ounce) package rice Chex
1 (16-ounce) package wheat Chex
1 (14-ounce) package pretzels (sticks,
   twists or rounds)
1 (12-ounce) can peanuts

Pour the oil into a large plastic food storage bag and shake to coat the side evenly. Add the dressing mix and shake well. Add the Bugles, crackers, cereal, pretzels and peanuts and shake to coat well. Store in a large airtight container.

Patti Reedy
Vera Bradley Sales Representative
Granddaughter of Vera Bradley

Spicy Pecans

YIELD: 8 SERVINGS

For a snack or in a salad, these are delicious!

2 large egg whites
1 1/2 teaspoons salt
3/4 cup sugar
2 teaspoons Worcestershire sauce
2 tablespoons hot paprika

1 1/2 teaspoons cayenne pepper
4 1/2 cups pecan halves
6 tablespoons unsalted butter, melted,
   cooled

Beat the egg whites and salt in a large mixing bowl until foamy. Add the sugar, Worcestershire sauce, paprika and cayenne pepper and beat well. Fold in the pecans and butter. Spread evenly on a nonstick baking sheet. Bake at 350 degrees for 30 to 40 minutes or until golden brown, stirring every 10 minutes. Let stand until cool. Store in an airtight container.

Nancy Graham
Vera Bradley Customer Service—Retired

Eggnog

4 cups milk
1/2 cup sugar
3 egg yolks
1/4 teaspoon salt
3 egg whites

1/4 cup sugar
1/8 teaspoon salt
1 teaspoon vanilla extract
Nutmeg to taste

Scald the milk in a saucepan until a thermometer registers 180 degrees. Let cool. Mix 1/2 cup sugar, egg yolks and 1/4 teaspoon salt in a double boiler. Add 1 cup of the milk and blend well. Stir in the remaining milk. Cook until the mixture coats a spoon, stirring frequently. Let stand until cool. Chill, covered, for 4 hours or longer before serving.

To serve, beat the egg whites in a mixing bowl until stiff peaks form. Fold into the milk mixture. Add 1/4 cup sugar, 1/8 teaspoon salt and vanilla and blend well. Sprinkle with nutmeg just before serving. Recipe may be frozen.

Sue Britton
Vera Bradley Marketing Manager

Sunny Day Sangria

This is a refreshing and light drink, perfect for a summer party, the beach or deck. The first time, I followed the recipe closely. Never having had sangria before, I mashed the fruit to a pulp and left it in. A friend later told me it only needed a light pressing to extract the juice. However, everyone at the party loved it. You decide either way.

1 orange, thinly sliced
1 lemon, thinly sliced
2 tablespoons confectioners' sugar
1 cup grape juice

4 cups cranberry juice cocktail
2 bottles dry red wine
2 cups club soda

Place the orange and lemon in a large serving bowl. Sprinkle with the confectioners' sugar. Mash the fruit lightly. Stir in the grape juice and cranberry juice cocktail. Chill until serving time. Add the wine and club soda just before serving. You may serve over ice.

Amy Grinsfelder
Vera Bradley Marketing Design Coordinator

Champagne Punch

Perfect for a bridal shower or any festive occasion.

1 lemon, thinly sliced	4 ounces apricot brandy
1 orange, thinly sliced	4 bottles Champagne
1 quart fresh strawberries, hulled	1 pint club soda
4 ounces brandy	4 (5-inch) pieces cucumber peel

Fill a ring mold with water and freeze until firm. Place the lemon, orange and strawberries in a large punch bowl. Add the brandy, apricot brandy, Champagne and club soda. Unmold the ice ring and place in the punch bowl. Garnish with the cucumber peels.

Amy Grinsfelder
Vera Bradley Marketing Design Coordinator

Grapefruit Margaritas

YIELD: 9 TO 12 SERVINGS

4 cups fresh grapefruit juice	3/4 cup Grand Marnier
Juice of 3 limes	1 cup sugar
2 cups tequila	

Mix the grapefruit juice, lime juice, tequila, Grand Marnier and sugar in a pitcher. Fill a blender container with crushed ice. Add 1/3 of the juice mixture. Process at high speed until frothy. Pour into 3 or 4 chilled or salt-rimmed glasses. Repeat 2 more times. Garnish each serving with a slice of lime and a sprig of mint.

Melanie Mauger
Vera Bradley Customer Service

Sparkling Raspberry Lemonade

1 (12-ounce) package frozen
   unsweetened raspberries, or
   3 cups fresh raspberries
1 cup sugar

1/2 cup water
1 1/2 tablespoons lemon zest
1 cup fresh lemon juice
1 (1-liter) bottle club soda

Combine the raspberries, sugar and water in a medium saucepan. Cook over medium heat until the sugar dissolves, stirring constantly. Increase heat to high and bring to a boil. Boil for 3 to 4 minutes. Strain into a bowl, discarding the solids. Add the lemon zest and mix well. Chill, covered, in the refrigerator.

    Combine the raspberry syrup mixture, lemon juice and club soda in a large pitcher and blend well. Serve over ice in glasses. Garnish the drink with fresh raspberries and place a slice of lemon on the edge of each glass.

Stacie Gray
Vera Bradley Customer Service

Santa's Cocoa Mix

YIELD: 7 CUPS MIX

Great holiday gift idea: place Santa's Cocoa Mix in a glass container decorated with Christmas ribbon, a measuring scoop and the recipe.

1 (8-ounce) package powdered milk
1 (6-ounce) jar powdered creamer

1 (2-pound) package Nestlé Quik
1 cup confectioners' sugar

Combine the powdered milk, powdered creamer, cocoa drink mix and confectioners' sugar in a large bowl and mix well. Store in an airtight container. To serve, dissolve 2 heaping spoonfuls of the mixture in 1 cup hot water.

Kathy Reedy Ray
Vera Bradley Marketing Associate
Granddaughter of Vera Bradley

Irish Crème

YIELD: 20 SERVINGS

Snuggle up to the fire with this delightful drink.

2 cups half-and-half
1 (14-ounce) can sweetened
*   condensed milk*
3 eggs

2 tablespoons chocolate syrup
1 tablespoon vanilla extract
1 cup whiskey
1/3 cup light rum

Process the half-and-half, condensed milk, eggs, chocolate syrup, vanilla, whiskey and rum in a blender for 1 minute. Serve with hot coffee.

Katrina Kay
Friend of Vera Bradley Designs

Warm Spiced Tea

YIELD: 24 SERVINGS

Serve this simply yummy tea on a chilly night.

Juice and zest of 6 oranges
Juice and zest of 4 lemons
2 cinnamon sticks

2 gallons water
16 tea bags
1¹/₂ cups honey

Combine the juices and zests in a large stockpot. Add the cinnamon sticks, water and tea bags. Bring to a boil over medium heat. Remove from heat and steep for 20 minutes. Strain, returning the liquid to the stockpot. Return to medium heat. Stir in the honey. Serve hot.

Kerry Reedy
Friend of Vera Bradley

Hot Cranberry Tea

YIELD: 12 TO 15 SERVINGS

This delicious tea is like no other tea you've ever had! Fresh cranberries give it a wonderful flavor, and all that vitamin C can sure chase away the chills.

1 (12-ounce) package fresh
  cranberries
2 cinnamon sticks
12 cups water

6 tablespoons lemon juice
1¹/₂ cups orange juice
1 to 2 cups sugar

Boil the cranberries and cinnamon sticks in the water in a large stockpot for 10 minutes. Cover and steep for 15 minutes. Strain, allowing some pulp to remain in the drink. Add the lemon juice, orange juice and sugar and mix well. Serve hot.

Sue Britton
Vera Bradley Marketing Manager

It's The Little Things

Soups, Salads & Sides

Southwest Roasted Red Pepper Bisque

Serve this very pretty soup around the holidays—especially when you have houseguests.

1/3 cup fresh cilantro, finely chopped
1/4 cup reduced-fat sour cream
2 teaspoons milk
1/2 teaspoon salt
2 teaspoons olive oil
2 cups chopped onions
1/2 cup chopped carrot
1 1/2 pounds red bell peppers, roasted, peeled, chopped (about 3 large)
1 tablespoon tomato paste

1/2 teaspoon cumin
1/4 teaspoon chili powder
1/8 teaspoon ground red pepper
2 garlic cloves, minced
3/4 cup cooked long grain rice
1/2 cup water
2 (10-ounce) cans chicken broth
1/2 cup milk
1/4 teaspoon salt
1/8 teaspoon black pepper

Combine the cilantro, sour cream, 2 teaspoons milk and 1/2 teaspoon salt in a small bowl and mix well.

Heat the oil in a Dutch oven over medium heat. Add the onions and carrot. Sauté until light brown. Stir in the roasted peppers, tomato paste, cumin, chili powder, red pepper and garlic. Cook for 5 minutes, stirring frequently. Stir in the rice, water and broth. Bring to a boil. Cover partially and reduce heat. Simmer for 15 minutes.

Process in batches in a food processor until smooth. Return to the Dutch oven. Stir in 1/2 cup milk, 1/4 teaspoon salt and black pepper. Cook over medium heat until heated through; do not boil. Ladle into soup bowls and top with the sour cream mixture.

Cheri Lantz
Vera Bradley Sales Analyst

Fresh Corn Chowder

YIELD: 4 SERVINGS

This is one of our all-time favorites at Vera Bradley.

1 medium onion, finely chopped
3 tablespoons butter
1 rib celery, finely chopped
1/4 green bell pepper, finely chopped
1/4 red bell pepper, finely chopped
2 or 3 red potatoes, chopped
2 tablespoons flour
1/2 teaspoon marjoram

1/2 teaspoon basil
1/4 teaspoon crushed sage
2 cups chicken broth
2 cups fresh corn kernels
   (about 4 ears)
1 1/2 cups light cream
1/2 cup milk
Salt and freshly ground pepper to taste

Sauté the onion in the butter in a Dutch oven over medium heat until tender. Add the celery, bell peppers and potatoes. Cook for 5 minutes, stirring occasionally. Stir in the flour. Cook for 2 minutes. Add the herbs and broth. Simmer, covered, over low heat for 30 minutes or until the potatoes are tender. Stir in the corn, cream, milk, salt and pepper. Cook until heated through; do not boil. Ladle immediately into soup bowls. Garnish with bacon bits and parsley.

Bonnie Stewart Mickelson
Friend of Vera Bradley Designs

Mushroom and Artichoke Soup

YIELD: 4 SERVINGS

An excellent starter for a dinner party.

3 tablespoons butter
1 cup thinly sliced mushrooms
1/2 cup finely chopped onion
2 tablespoons flour
2 1/2 cups half-and-half
1 1/2 cups chicken broth

1 (14-ounce) can artichoke hearts,
   drained, chopped
Salt to taste
Cayenne pepper to taste
Beau Monde seasoning to taste

Melt the butter in a large saucepan over medium-high heat. Add the mushrooms and onion. Sauté for 5 minutes or until golden brown. Stir in the flour. Cook for 2 minutes over low heat. Add the half-and-half and broth gradually, stirring constantly. Cook over low heat until thickened, stirring constantly. Stir in the artichokes and seasonings to taste. Ladle into large soup bowls. Garnish with additional sliced fresh mushrooms and sprigs of parsley.

Kim Colby
Vera Bradley Vice President of Design

Swiss Onion Soup

Swiss Onion Soup is heartier than French onion soup and it is fabulous.

2 pounds onions, thinly sliced
1/3 cup butter
2 tablespoons finely chopped garlic
2 tablespoons dry mustard
2 to 3 tablespoons crushed sage
6 cups chicken or beef broth
1/4 cup dry red wine

1/3 cup butter
2/3 cup flour
1 cup heavy cream
Salt and pepper to taste
Croutons
Swiss cheese slices
Grated Parmesan cheese

Sauté the onions in 1/3 cup butter in a Dutch oven until dark golden brown. Add the garlic, dry mustard and sage. Stir in the broth and wine.

Melt 1/3 cup butter in a medium saucepan. Whisk in the flour. Cook until light brown, whisking constantly. Add the cream. Cook until smooth, whisking constantly. Stir into the onion mixture. Bring to a boil. Cook for 1 minute. Season with salt and pepper. Ladle into soup bowls. Top with croutons, Swiss cheese and Parmesan cheese.

Stacie Gray
Vera Bradley Customer Service

Potato Cheese Soup

YIELD: 4 SERVINGS

This is one cozy bowl of soup! Add slippers and a fire
for a perfect winter supper.

4 cups chopped peeled potatoes
1 1/2 cups water
2 teaspoons salt
1 tablespoon olive oil
1 onion, chopped
1 3/4 to 2 cups milk

1 cup shredded Cheddar cheese
2 tablespoons butter
1/2 teaspoon pepper
1/8 teaspoon minced garlic
Parsley to taste

Combine the potatoes, water and salt in a saucepan. Cook for 20 minutes or until tender; do not drain. Heat the oil in a small skillet. Add the onion. Sauté for 10 minutes or until translucent.

Purée the undrained potatoes and onion in a food processor or blender. Pour into a large saucepan. Cook over medium heat until heated through. Add enough milk to make of the desired consistency. Stir in the cheese, butter, pepper, garlic and parsley. Cook until heated through. You may add one 10-ounce package frozen peas for a new twist.

Sue Britton
Vera Bradley Marketing Manager

Squash Soup

YIELD: 6 TO 8 SERVINGS

My friend Joanne gave me this recipe. She makes it for her husband, who is on a very strict low-fat diet. This soup is very rich, yet is low in cholesterol. The recipe calls for nonfat evaporated milk, but you can use regular low-fat milk if you wish. This is a great soup for Thanksgiving.

1 onion, chopped
1 shallot, sliced
1 leek, sliced
1 (14-ounce) can chicken broth

1 acorn squash, cooked, peeled
1 butternut squash, cooked, peeled
1 cup nonfat evaporated milk or
    1% milk

Sauté the onion, shallot and leek in a nonstick skillet until tender. Add the broth and cooked squash. Simmer for 30 minutes. Purée in a food processor or blender. Stir in the evaporated milk. Ladle into soup bowls. Garnish with a dollop of sour cream and toasted almonds.

Cookie Leiber
Friend of Vera Bradley Designs

Vera's Beefy Vegetable Soup

YIELD: 4 TO 6 SERVINGS

Whenever I visited Vera and Ed in Florida, I could always count
on a pot of homemade soup simmering on the stove—especially after a
late-night flight. Here is one of Vera's concoctions.

2 pounds ground beef
2 to 3 carrots, peeled, chopped
2 potatoes, peeled, chopped
1 onion, chopped
1 small head cabbage, cored, shredded
4 ribs celery, chopped

4 cups vegetable juice cocktail
1 bay leaf, or to taste
Garlic powder, oregano and parsley
   to taste
Salt and pepper to taste

Brown the ground beef in a skillet, stirring until crumbly; drain. Combine
the vegetables with water to cover in a large stockpot. Add the vegetable
juice cocktail, bay leaf and seasonings to taste. Stir in the ground beef. Simmer
for 30 minutes. Discard the bay leaf. Serve immediately.

Betty Genter
Vera Bradley's Niece

Grocery Shopper's Soup

YIELD: 4 TO 6 SERVINGS

I call this soup Grocery Shopper's Soup because a fellow shopper told me
about it in the checkout line. It couldn't be easier—and it is really good.

4 Italian sausages
1 (14-ounce) can whole tomatoes
1 (16-ounce) can chicken broth
1 (16-ounce) can spinach or
   turnip greens

1 (16-ounce) can red kidney beans
1 (16-ounce) can sliced potatoes
1 (8-ounce) can sliced carrots
1 teaspoon vinegar

Cook the sausages in the casings in a skillet until cooked through. Cut
into slices.

Drain the tomatoes, reserving the juice. Chop the tomatoes coarsely.
Combine the sliced sausages, broth, tomatoes, reserved juice, undrained
vegetables and vinegar in a large saucepan. Simmer over medium heat for
30 minutes. Serve immediately.

Dorothy McAfee
Cynthia's at Palatka Office Supply
Palatka, Florida

Tucson Soup

This is a thick, hearty soup that is quite satisfying and easy to prepare.
It's great served in Italian bread bowls.

2 tablespoons olive oil
4 or 5 unpeeled red potatoes, chopped
2 or 3 carrots, chopped
1 onion, chopped
2 (14-ounce) cans chicken broth
1 cup water

1/4 teaspoon marjoram
1/4 teaspoon basil
1 small bay leaf
1/8 teaspoon pepper
1 (16-ounce) can white kidney beans
2/3 cup ditalini or tubetti macaroni

Heat the oil in a 4-quart saucepan over medium-high heat. Add the potatoes, carrots and onion. Cook for 5 minutes, stirring frequently. Add the broth, water, marjoram, basil, bay leaf and pepper. Bring to a boil and reduce heat to low. Simmer for 30 minutes.

Bring the undrained beans and macaroni to a boil in a medium saucepan over medium heat and reduce heat to low. Simmer, covered, for 15 minutes, stirring occasionally. Stir into the potato mixture. Simmer for 10 to 15 minutes. Discard the bay leaf before serving.

Betty Howell
Country Classics
Keyser, West Virginia

Chunky Minestrone

Although we have no Italian in our family background, we could never convince my husband Jay of this. After years of running his own Italian restaurant, he still enjoys the food. This easy and hearty soup is one of our favorites.

2 teaspoons olive oil
1¹/2 cups chopped onions
1 medium carrot, cut into halves
    lengthwise, chopped
1 garlic clove, minced
2 (14-ounce) cans chopped Italian
    tomatoes
1 (10-ounce) can chicken broth
2¹/2 cups water
1 teaspoon Italian seasoning

1 medium zucchini, cut into halves
    lengthwise, sliced
1 (15-ounce) can cannellini, drained
1 (10-ounce) package frozen chopped
    spinach, thawed, drained
8 ounces uncooked bow tie pasta
¹/4 teaspoon salt
¹/4 teaspoon pepper
²/3 cup grated Parmesan cheese

Heat the oil in a Dutch oven over medium-high heat. Add the onions, carrot and garlic. Sauté for 3 minutes. Add the undrained tomatoes, broth, water and Italian seasoning. Bring to a boil. Cover and reduce heat to medium-low. Simmer for 20 minutes. Add the zucchini, beans, spinach, pasta, salt and pepper. Cook for 7 to 10 minutes or until the pasta is al dente. Ladle into soup bowls. Sprinkle with the Parmesan cheese.

Joan Bradley Reedy
Vera Bradley Sales Representative
Daughter of Vera Bradley

Hearty Tortellini Vegetable Soup

YIELD: 4 TO 6 SERVINGS

Believe it or not, this is a diet recipe that we have doctored up a bit—not in fat, but only in spices and more vegetables.

1 cup chopped onion
1 cup chopped carrots
2 garlic cloves, minced
4 teaspoons olive or vegetable oil
3 cups quartered mushrooms
1 cup sliced zucchini
4 cups spinach leaves, rinsed, drained

3 cups canned stewed tomatoes
2 cups canned chicken broth
2 tablespoons chopped fresh parsley
2 tablespoons chopped fresh dillweed
   or basil
2 cups frozen cheese-filled tortellini

Sauté the onion, carrots and garlic in the oil in a large stockpot for 10 minutes or until tender. Add the mushrooms and zucchini. Sauté for 10 minutes. Add the spinach, tomatoes, broth, parsley and dillweed. Simmer, covered, for 30 to 40 minutes. Stir in the pasta. Cook for 10 to 15 minutes or until heated through.

Kathy Reedy Ray
Vera Bradley Marketing Associate
Granddaughter of Vera Bradley

Mom's Chili

YIELD: 10 TO 12 SERVINGS

If you already have a favorite chili recipe, try this one. We think you will love ours even more.

3 pounds ground beef
2 large onions, chopped
6 garlic cloves, chopped
2 (6-ounce) cans tomato paste
3 (8-ounce) cans tomato sauce
4 tomato sauce cans water
2 medium cans tomato juice

2 (15-ounce) cans Mexican
   chili beans
5 tablespoons chili powder
1 tablespoon cumin
$1/2$ tablespoon oregano
Tabasco sauce to taste
Salt and pepper to taste

Brown the ground beef in a large skillet, stirring until crumbly; drain.
   Combine the ground beef, onions, garlic, tomato paste, tomato sauce, water, tomato juice, beans, chili powder, cumin, oregano, Tabasco sauce, salt and pepper in a large stockpot. Bring to a boil and reduce heat. Simmer for 2 hours. You may prepare 24 hours in advance to enhance the flavor.

Sharon Keogh
Monograms and More
Hinsdale, Illinois

Chicken Chili

If the way to a man's heart is through his stomach,
this one will surely hit the spot.

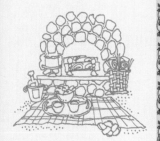

3 tablespoons olive oil
1 1/2 pounds boneless skinless chicken
  breasts, chopped
1 cup chopped onion
3 garlic cloves, minced
1 red bell pepper, chopped
1 1/2 teaspoons cumin seeds
2 tablespoons olive oil
1 (10-ounce) can tomatoes with
  green chiles
1 (23-ounce) can tomato sauce

1 (12-ounce) can beer
1 tablespoon chili powder
1 teaspoon oregano
1/8 teaspoon salt
1/8 teaspoon pepper
2 (16-ounce) cans black beans,
  drained
1 (10-ounce) package frozen corn
1/2 cup sliced black olives
2 teaspoons minced cilantro
2 cups shredded Cheddar cheese

Heat 3 tablespoons oil in a Dutch oven. Add the chicken. Sauté for 4 minutes or until cooked through. Remove from the Dutch oven to a warm plate. Wipe the Dutch oven clean with a paper towel. Sauté the onion, garlic, bell pepper and cumin seeds in 2 tablespoons oil in the Dutch oven. Add the tomatoes, tomato sauce, beer, chili powder, oregano, salt and pepper and mix well. Add the chicken. Simmer, covered, for 20 minutes. Add the black beans, corn and black olives. Simmer for 15 minutes. Stir in the cilantro. Ladle into soup bowls. Sprinkle with the cheese.

Kim Colby
Vera Bradley Vice President of Design

For a delicious presentation, serve Chicken Chili in warm, crusty bread bowls. For a fall picnic or tailgate party, use traditional onion soup bowls with handles— it's a great way to manage a hot bowl of soup in the great outdoors! For a cool weather menu idea, start off with a good beer or light white wine and Beer Cheese Dip (page 35). Pair Chicken Chili with Wine Lovers' Salad (page 79) and corn bread and, for dessert, try Aunt Franny's Apple Cake (page 173) with a cup of Warm Spiced Tea (page 53). Spread a blanket on the ground (even if you're inside by the fire!) and sprinkle generously with colorful fall leaves for a beautifully simple "table setting!"

Killer White Chili

1 pound boneless skinless chicken
  breasts, cooked, chopped
1 (48-ounce) jar Great Northern
  beans
1 (16-ounce) jar salsa

8 ounces Monterey Jack cheese with
  jalapeño chiles, shredded
1/2 cup chicken broth
1 (12-ounce) can beer (optional)
2 teaspoons cumin

Combine the chicken, beans, salsa, cheese, broth, beer and cumin in a slow
cooker. Cook on Low for 4 to 5 hours. Serve with corn bread or tortilla chips.

Thirza Youker
Vera Bradley Customer Service—Retired

Chicken Soup with Ricotta Dumplings

This was the first "serious recipe" that I made for my boyfriend Bill. I guess it
worked . . . we were married in my mother's garden on June 12, 1999!

13 cups (or more) chicken stock
2 carrots, thinly chopped
2 ribs celery with leaves, thinly sliced
1 large yellow onion, chopped
2 tablespoons finely chopped
  fresh parsley
2 teaspoons salt
1/2 teaspoon freshly ground pepper
2 cups flour, sifted

1 tablespoon baking powder
1 teaspoon salt
2 eggs
1/2 cup part-skim ricotta cheese
1/4 cup low-fat milk
1 tablespoon finely chopped
  fresh thyme
1 tablespoon finely chopped
  fresh parsley

Combine 13 cups stock, carrots, celery, onion and 2 tablespoons parsley in a
large stockpot. Bring to a boil over medium heat and reduce heat. Simmer
while making the dumplings, adding additional stock if needed to always
maintain a depth of 4 inches of liquid. Season with 2 teaspoons salt and pepper.
　Sift the flour, baking powder and 1 teaspoon salt into a medium bowl.
Combine the eggs, ricotta cheese, milk, thyme and 1 tablespoon parsley in a
small bowl and mix well. Add to the flour mixture and stir just until the dough
holds together. Shape the dough into dumplings using a tablespoon. Drop into
the simmering stock mixture. Simmer for 15 minutes.

Debra Bleeke
Vera Bradley Customer Service

Wildwood's Famous Chicken Tortilla Soup

YIELD: 4 TO 6 SERVINGS

The best thing about this soup, other than the taste, is the
only thing you have to cut up is the chicken.

3 or 4 boneless skinless chicken breasts
3 (14-ounce) cans tomatoes with
  green chiles
1 (14-ounce) can diced tomatoes
1 (30-ounce) can white or golden
  hominy
1 (16-ounce) can pinto beans

1 (16-ounce) can dark red kidney
  beans
1 envelope taco seasoning mix
1 envelope ranch salad dressing mix
White tortilla chips
Shredded Monterey Jack cheese

Boil the chicken in water to cover in a large stockpot until cooked through.
Drain the chicken, reserving 4 cups of the broth. Cool the chicken slightly
and shred.

Combine the chicken, reserved broth, tomatoes with green chiles,
tomatoes, hominy, pinto beans, kidney beans, taco seasoning mix and ranch
salad dressing mix in the stockpot. Bring to a boil and reduce heat. Simmer for
30 minutes. Ladle into soup bowls. Sprinkle with white tortilla chips and
shredded Monterey Jack cheese.

Dana Manning
Wildwood Tennis Club

Wish'n Well Chicken Soup

YIELD: 8 SERVINGS

1 (3¹/2- to 4-pound) whole chicken
10 cups cold water
2 chicken bouillon cubes
2 large onions, quartered
¹/4 small cabbage
¹/2 cup chopped parsley
3 ribs celery with leaves,
   cut into pieces

2 garlic cloves
10 peppercorns
1 bay leaf
3 sprigs fresh thyme, or ¹/2 teaspoon
   dried thyme
¹/8 teaspoon tarragon
¹/4 cup barley, or 4 ounces pasta
2 cups carrots, sliced

Place the chicken in the cold water in a stockpot. Bring to a boil. Skim the surface. Add the bouillon cubes, onions, cabbage, parsley, celery, garlic, peppercorns, bay leaf, thyme and tarragon. Simmer for 1¹/2 hours. Cool slightly. Drain the chicken, reserving the broth and discarding the vegetables and whole seasonings. Cut the chicken into bite-size pieces, discarding the skin and bones. Chill the broth and chicken in separate covered containers in the refrigerator.

    Skim the surface of the broth. Place the broth in a stockpot. Bring to a simmer over medium heat. Add the barley. Simmer, covered, for 45 minutes. Add the carrots and chicken. Simmer for 15 minutes or until heated through. You may use 3 chicken breasts, 3 thighs and 3 drumsticks instead of the whole chicken.

Marilyn Neil
Wish'n Well Gift Shop
Buffalo, New York

Clam Chowder

4 ounces bacon
1 onion, chopped
6 potatoes, peeled, chopped
1 1/2 cups clam juice
2 (7-ounce) cans clams
2 chicken bouillon cubes
1 teaspoon salt

3/4 teaspoon Worcestershire sauce
1/2 teaspoon Tabasco sauce
1/4 teaspoon white pepper
6 tablespoons butter
1 cup flour
5 cups half-and-half or milk

Fry the bacon in a heavy stockpot until crisp. Remove the bacon to paper towels to drain. Add the onion to the drippings in the stockpot. Sauté for 5 minutes. Add the potatoes, clam juice, undrained clams, bouillon cubes, salt, Worcestershire sauce, Tabasco sauce and white pepper. Simmer for 30 minutes. Reduce heat to low.

Melt the butter in a saucepan. Whisk in the flour to form a roux. Add the half-and-half. Cook for 10 minutes or until thickened, stirring constantly. Add to the clam mixture. Crumble the bacon and add to the chowder. Simmer over medium-low heat for 10 minutes. Ladle into soup bowls. Garnish with oyster crackers and fresh parsley.

Joanie Byrne Hall
Granddaughter of Vera Bradley

Pistachio-Crusted Goat Cheese with Fresh Orange Vinaigrette

YIELD: 4 SERVINGS

This is best served as a side salad teamed with a beef or pork entrée.

1/2 cup shelled pistachios
4 ounces goat cheese
3 cups mixed salad greens
1 small red onion, sliced

Fresh Orange Vinaigrette (below)
Sections of 1 to 2 oranges
1 cup red raspberries

Toast the pistachios in a preheated nonstick skillet over medium heat, stirring constantly and removing from heat occasionally to prevent burning. Remove from heat and cool. Place on a cutting board and crush with a rolling pin.

Cut the goat cheese into 8 slices 1/2 inch thick, reshaping into slices if the cheese crumbles. Dip into the pistachios, coating both sides.

Toss the salad greens with the onion slices in a salad bowl. Drizzle with Fresh Orange Vinaigrette and toss to coat.

Place the cheese on a microwave-safe plate. Microwave on High for 20 seconds or until warm.

To serve, place the salad green mixture on individual serving plates. Arrange the orange sections and raspberries on each portion. Place 2 cheese slices on each plate. Serve immediately.

Fresh Orange Vinaigrette

YIELD: 4 CUPS

2 to 3 oranges
1 cup vegetable oil
1 cup olive oil
3/4 cup red wine vinegar

1 cup fresh orange juice (juice of
  3 to 4 oranges)
1 teaspoon salt
Pepper to taste

Remove the peel from the oranges, reserving the pulp for another purpose. Pulse the orange peel in a food processor 5 or 6 times or until finely ground. Measure 1/4 cup of the ground orange peel, reserving any remaining peel for another purpose.

Combine the vegetable oil, olive oil, vinegar, orange juice, ground orange peel, salt and pepper in a large bottle with a tight-fitting lid. Cover and shake well.

Kathy Miller
Vera Bradley Classic Steering Committee

Mandarin Orange and Lettuce Salad

Easy and pretty!

6 slices bacon
2 large heads Bibb or Boston lettuce
1 (8-ounce) can mandarin oranges,
   drained

1/4 cup almonds, toasted
Vinaigrette (below)

Cook the bacon in a skillet until crisp. Remove to paper towels to drain. Crumble the bacon.

Tear the lettuce into bite-size pieces into a large salad bowl. Add the oranges, almonds and bacon. Toss with enough Vinaigrette to coat. You may add sliced celery and green onions if desired.

Vinaigrette

1 cup salad oil
1/4 cup vinegar
2 teaspoons salt
1 teaspoon paprika

1 teaspoon pepper
1/4 teaspoon dry mustard
1/4 teaspoon confectioners' sugar

Combine the oil, vinegar, salt, paprika, pepper, dry mustard and confectioners' sugar in a container with a tight-fitting lid. Cover and shake well. Chill until ready to use. You may store in the refrigerator for several weeks.

Sharon Keogh
Monograms & More
Hinsdale, Illinois

Salad with Pears, Walnuts and Bleu Cheese

YIELD: 6 SERVINGS

1 small garlic clove, minced
1/8 to 1/4 teaspoon salt
1/3 cup red wine vinegar
1 teaspoon lemon juice
1 shallot, minced
1 teaspoon Dijon mustard
1 teaspoon lemon zest

2 teaspoons cracked black peppercorns
1 cup olive oil
1 1/2 heads green leaf lettuce,
    torn into bite-size pieces
2 large pears, peeled, sliced
1 cup walnut pieces, toasted
3/4 cup crumbled bleu cheese

Mash the garlic and salt in a bowl to form a paste. Add the vinegar, lemon juice, shallot, Dijon mustard, lemon zest and black peppercorns and whisk well. Add the oil in a fine stream, whisking constantly.

Arrange the lettuce on 6 individual salad plates. Divide the pears, walnuts and bleu cheese equally among the plates. Drizzle with the vinaigrette. Serve immediately.

Susie Bruce
Vera Bradley Merchandising Coordinator—Retired

Pear, Watercress and Endive Salad with Sweet Gorgonzola

YIELD: 6 SERVINGS

The bitterness of the endive and the sweetness of the
cheese create a perfect balance in this salad.

2 heads Belgian endive, julienned
2 bunches watercress, trimmed
2 pears, cored, chopped
1/4 cup white wine vinegar
1 teaspoon prepared mustard

1 tablespoon minced fresh parsley
1/2 cup olive oil
4 ounces crumbled sweet Gorgonzola
    cheese

Combine the endive, watercress and pears in a large salad bowl and toss to mix well.

Combine the vinegar, mustard and parsley in a bowl. Add the oil in a fine stream, whisking constantly until blended. Pour over the salad mixture and toss to coat. Sprinkle with the cheese.

Cookie Leiber
Friend of Vera Bradley Designs

Salad with Strawberries and Almonds

YIELD: 4 SERVINGS

This is a nice spring salad when strawberries are at their best.

6 cups mixed salad greens
1 cup fresh strawberries, sliced
3/4 cup crumbled bleu cheese

1/2 cup slivered almonds
3/4 cup poppy seed salad dressing

Divide the salad greens among 4 salad plates. Arrange the strawberries and bleu cheese on each salad. Sprinkle with almonds. Drizzle with the salad dressing. Serve immediately. You may sprinkle with garlic and herb croutons for an added crunch.

Patti Reedy
Vera Bradley Sales Representative
Granddaughter of Vera Bradley

Asparagus Salad

YIELD: 4 SERVINGS

Chill this salad for at least four hours before serving.

2 pounds fresh asparagus, cut into
    4-inch pieces
1/2 cup olive oil
2 tablespoons red wine vinegar
2 teaspoons chopped parsley

1/4 teaspoon salt
1/4 teaspoon freshly ground pepper
Yolk of 1 hard-cooked egg, crumbled
1 tablespoon capers, drained
6 to 8 large black olives

Steam the asparagus over boiling water in a steamer for 5 to 7 minutes or until tender-crisp. Place in a shallow dish.

Combine the oil, vinegar, parsley, salt and pepper in a bowl and mix well. Pour over the asparagus. Marinate, covered, in the refrigerator for 4 hours or longer.

To serve, drain the asparagus and place on a serving platter. Sprinkle the egg yolk over the bottom of the stalks and the capers over the top. Garnish with the black olives. Serve at room temperature.

Katrina Kay
Friend of Vera Bradley Designs

If your salad recipe calls for mixed greens and you cannot find them pre-packaged at your grocer, try a small combination of any of these for that added "punch:"

Spinach—Whether curly or smooth leaves, make sure they are crisp and dark.

Frisée—Lacy and pale green with firm, white ribs. Slightly bitter, so use sparingly.

Radicchio—Beautiful, deep crimson leaves and white ribs bring a wonderful taste and color to any salad.

Belgian Endive—A member of the chicory family, these spear-shaped shoots are tinted yellow. Over-exposure to light will turn them dark and bitter.

Caesar Salad

The bleu cheese is a nice addition to this version of Caesar salad.

1 large head romaine
1 garlic clove
1/2 cup salad oil
6 anchovy fillets, drained, chopped
1 1/2 teaspoons Worcestershire sauce
3/4 teaspoon salt
1/4 teaspoon dry mustard

1/4 teaspoon freshly ground pepper
1 egg
1/4 cup crumbled bleu cheese
2 tablespoons grated Parmesan cheese
2 tablespoons lemon juice
1 cup Caesar salad croutons

Trim the core from the lettuce and separate the leaves. Rinse under cold water and shake to drain. Pat dry with paper towels. Wrap in plastic wrap. Chill for several hours.

Cut the garlic into halves. Reserve 1 half of the garlic. Crush the remaining garlic. Combine with the oil, anchovies, Worcestershire sauce, salt, dry mustard and pepper in a jar with a tight-fitting lid. Cover and shake vigorously. Chill until serving time.

Rub the reserved garlic inside a wooden salad bowl; discard the garlic. Cut out the large ribs from the large leaves of the romaine. Tear the leaves into bite-size pieces and place in the prepared salad bowl.

To serve, bring 2 inches of water to a boil in a small saucepan. Turn off heat. Lower the egg carefully into the water. Let stand for 1 minute; drain. Shake the dressing and pour over the romaine. Sprinkle with the bleu cheese and Parmesan cheese and toss to coat well. Break the egg over the center of the salad. Pour the lemon juice over the egg. Toss the salad to coat well. Sprinkle with the croutons and toss quickly. Serve immediately.

Sharon Keogh
Monograms & More
Hinsdale, Illinois

Cashew Pea Salad

1/2 cup sour cream
1 cup prepared ranch salad dressing
1 (10-ounce) package frozen baby
  peas, thawed
1 cup chopped celery

1 cup cauliflower florets
1/2 cup sliced green onions
8 ounces bacon, cooked, crumbled
1 cup cashew halves

Mix the sour cream and ranch dressing in a bowl. Combine the peas, celery, cauliflower, green onions and bacon in a large serving bowl and mix well. Add the dressing mixture and toss to coat well. Chill, covered, until serving time. Sprinkle with the cashews just before serving.

Joan Bond
Vera Bradley Classic Steering Committee

Green Bean and New Potato Salad

YIELD: 4 TO 6 SERVINGS

This salad makes a beautiful presentation at a family get-together.

1 1/2 pounds small red potatoes
1 pound green beans, trimmed
1 medium red onion, chopped
1/2 cup fresh basil, chopped
1/4 cup balsamic vinegar
2 tablespoons Dijon mustard

2 tablespoons fresh lemon juice
1 garlic clove, minced
1 teaspoon Worcestershire sauce
1/2 cup olive oil
Salt and pepper to taste

Steam the potatoes over boiling water in a steamer for 10 minutes. Cool and cut into quarters. Add the green beans to the steamer. Steam for 5 minutes or until tender-crisp. Place the green beans in ice water in a bowl to cool; drain. Cut the green beans into halves. Combine the green beans, potatoes, onion and basil in a large serving bowl.

Combine the vinegar, Dijon mustard, lemon juice, garlic and Worcestershire sauce in a medium bowl and whisk well. Add the oil gradually, whisking constantly. Season with salt and pepper. Pour over the vegetable mixture and toss to coat. Adjust the seasonings to taste. Serve at room temperature.

Stacie Gray
Vera Bradley Customer Service

Potato Salad

YIELD: 8 TO 10 SERVINGS

Guard the refrigerator! At our house, some of this always comes up missing during the "refrigerate overnight" part of the recipe . . .

1/2 cup (1 stick) margarine
10 large potatoes, cooked, chopped
Salt and pepper to taste
2 to 2 1/2 cups mayonnaise-type salad
  dressing
2 teaspoons prepared mustard
2 tablespoons vinegar

8 to 10 tablespoons sugar
Milk
1 medium onion, finely chopped
2 small carrots, finely chopped
6 hard-cooked eggs, chopped
1 (6-ounce) jar pitted green olives,
  drained, sliced

Melt the margarine in a large skillet. Add the potatoes, stirring to coat; do not brown. Remove from heat. Season with salt and pepper.

Combine the salad dressing, mustard, vinegar and sugar in a bowl and mix well. Add enough milk to make of the desired consistency.

Combine the onion, carrots, eggs and olives in a large serving bowl. Stir in the potatoes. Add the dressing and toss to coat. Chill, covered, for 8 to 12 hours.

Joan Bradley Reedy
Vera Bradley Sales Representative
Daughter of Vera Bradley

Roasted Red Pepper, Corn and Rice Salad

YIELD: 6 TO 8 SERVINGS

An excellent summer salad—sure to be made more than once a summer. It is best made with fresh sweet corn in season.

1 tablespoon margarine
1 1/2 cups long grain white rice
3 cups water
2 teaspoons salt
1/4 cup mayonnaise
1/2 cup buttermilk
1/3 cup grated Parmesan cheese
1 tablespoon red wine vinegar

2 cups fresh whole kernel corn or
  drained, thawed frozen whole
  kernel corn
1 (14-ounce) jar roasted red peppers,
  cut into 1/2-inch pieces
3/4 cup thinly sliced green onions
Salt and pepper to taste

Melt the margarine in a medium saucepan over medium-high heat. Add the rice. Sauté until almost brown. Add the water and 2 teaspoons salt. Cook for 20 minutes or until just tender, stirring until all of the liquid has been absorbed; holes will form in the rice. Spoon into a large bowl. Cool to room temperature. You may chill, covered, in the refrigerator to speed up the chilling process.

Whisk the mayonnaise in a large glass measure until smooth. Add the buttermilk, Parmesan cheese and vinegar and whisk to blend well.

Combine the rice, corn, roasted peppers and 1/2 cup of the green onions in a large serving bowl and mix well. Stir in the dressing and season with salt and pepper to taste. Sprinkle with the remaining 1/4 cup green onions. Serve at room temperature.

Stefanie Chevillet
Vera Bradley Customer Service

Chinese Coleslaw

This recipe is so simple. It's a great way to introduce
kids to salad! They'll love to make it.

1 (3-ounce) package Ramen Oodles
   of Noodles
Butter for sautéing
1 (16-ounce) package coleslaw mix
1 to 2 green onions, sliced

1/2 cup sunflower kernels
1/2 cup almonds
1/4 cup vegetable oil
3 tablespoons sugar
1/2 teaspoon salt

Sauté the noodles in butter in a skillet. Combine the coleslaw mix, green
onions, sunflower kernels, almonds and sautéed noodles in a large serving bowl
and toss to mix. Whisk the oil, sugar and salt in a bowl. Pour over the coleslaw
mixture and toss to coat. Chill, covered, for 45 minutes. Toss the coleslaw
before serving.

Judy Wintin
Vera Bradley Cutting Department Team

Super Slaw

YIELD: 8 SERVINGS

The dressing is really quite different—a nice change of
pace from traditional coleslaw.

6 tablespoons rice vinegar
6 tablespoons vegetable oil
5 tablespoons creamy peanut butter
3 tablespoons soy sauce
3 tablespoons light brown sugar
2 tablespoons minced peeled
   fresh gingerroot
1 1/2 tablespoons minced garlic

5 cups thinly sliced green cabbage
2 cups thinly sliced red cabbage
2 large red or yellow bell peppers,
   julienned
2 medium carrots, julienned
8 green onions, sliced
1/2 cup cilantro, chopped
Salt and pepper to taste

Combine the vinegar, oil, peanut butter, soy sauce, brown sugar, ginger and
garlic in a small bowl and whisk to blend well.
    Combine the cabbages, bell peppers, carrots, green onions and cilantro
in a large serving bowl. Add the dressing and toss to coat well. Season with
salt and pepper. You may prepare the dressing 24 hours before serving and
store, covered, in the refrigerator. Bring to room temperature before tossing
with the salad.

Lyn Killoran
Friend of Vera Bradley

Radish Salad

After years of gatherings and socials with the same old "radish roses" on the vegetable platters, we finally found a great recipe for this maligned vegetable.

1 cup sliced radishes
1/4 cup white vinegar
1 teaspoon salt
Olive oil

Freshly ground black pepper to taste
1 tablespoon capers, drained
1 canned chile pepper, cut into strips

Soak the radishes in a mixture of vinegar and salt in a small bowl for 3 hours or longer; drain. Arrange on 2 salad plates. Drizzle with oil and sprinkle with black pepper. Top with capers and chile pepper strips.

Patti Pine
Vera Bradley Sales Representative Coordinator

Spinach Salad with Hot Bacon Raspberry Vinaigrette

1 pound baby spinach, trimmed
1 cup thinly sliced fresh mushrooms
1 red onion, sliced, separated
  into rings
2 hard-cooked eggs, sliced
1 pound bacon, cut into small pieces
1/2 cup raspberry vinegar

1/4 cup Dijon mustard
2 tablespoons sugar
1/4 teaspoon Tabasco sauce or other
  hot sauce
1/2 cup olive oil
Freshly ground pepper to taste
1 cup fresh raspberries

Combine the spinach, mushrooms, onion rings and eggs in a large salad bowl.

Cook the bacon in a large skillet over medium-high heat until crisp. Drain the bacon, reserving 1 cup of the hot bacon drippings. Place the bacon on paper towels and pat dry. Crumble the bacon and add to the spinach mixture.

Process the vinegar, Dijon mustard, sugar and Tabasco sauce in a food processor. Add the reserved hot bacon drippings and oil separately in a fine stream, processing constantly. Adjust the seasonings to taste. Pour over the spinach mixture and toss to coat. Divide among 6 salad plates. Sprinkle with pepper and fresh raspberries.

Kim Colby
Vera Bradley Vice President of Design

Eight-Vegetable Marinated Salad

YIELD: 8 TO 10 SERVINGS

Great for a crowd or to bring to a potluck dinner,
this salad is always a favorite.

1 (16-ounce) can cut green beans,
   drained
1 (16-ounce) can cut wax beans,
   drained
1 (15-ounce) can kidney beans,
   drained
1 cup drained cooked lima beans
1 cup drained cooked whole
   kernel corn

1 (8-ounce) can sliced carrots,
   drained
3 medium red onions, chopped
2 medium green bell peppers, chopped
1 cup red cider vinegar
1 cup sugar
1/2 cup vegetable oil
Salt and pepper to taste

Combine the vegetables in a large bowl and toss gently. Bring the vinegar, sugar and oil to a boil in a saucepan. Pour over the vegetables and stir gently. Season with salt and pepper. Marinate, covered, in the refrigerator for 8 to 12 hours.

Denise Mitchell
Vera Bradley Administrative Assistant

Wine Lovers' Salad

YIELD: 4 SERVINGS

This is a simple salad that is great for a family dinner or
a larger event—just adjust the proportions.

1/2 cup olive oil
2 tablespoons red wine
1 1/2 tablespoons red wine vinegar
1 tablespoon Dijon mustard
1 teaspoon salt

3/4 teaspoon pepper
6 cups torn lettuce greens
1 cup shredded Swiss cheese
3/4 cup chopped walnut pieces

Combine the oil, wine, vinegar, Dijon mustard, salt and pepper in a salad cruet. Cover and shake vigorously.

    Combine the lettuce greens, cheese and walnuts in a salad bowl. Add the vinaigrette and toss to coat. Serve immediately.

Jill Nichols
Vera Bradley Executive Vice President/COO

Mexican Fiesta Salad

Serve this salad at a family gathering or a get-together
with friends—the presentation is spectacular.

$^1/_2$ cup dried black beans
2 tablespoons olive oil
2 tablespoons white wine vinegar
$^1/_2$ teaspoon salt
$^1/_2$ cup chopped red onion
1 cup whole kernel corn
$^1/_2$ cup chopped green bell pepper
2 cups thinly sliced romaine or
  red leaf lettuce

$1^1/_2$ cups chopped seeded tomatoes
1 cup shredded Monterey Jack cheese
1 ripe avocado
4 slices bacon, cooked, drained,
  crumbled
Cilantro Vinaigrette (page 81)

Rinse and sort the beans. Place in a large saucepan. Cover with 2 inches of
cold water. Bring to a boil. Boil for 3 minutes. Remove from heat. Soak for
10 minutes; drain. Cover the beans with 2 inches of cold water. Bring to a boil
and reduce heat. Simmer for 45 minutes or until tender; drain. Combine the
beans with the oil, vinegar and salt in a bowl and mix well. Marinate, covered,
in the refrigerator for 2 hours.

To serve, drain the beans. Combine the beans and onion in a bowl and mix
well. Mix the corn and bell pepper in a small bowl. Arrange the lettuce in a
large serving bowl. Reserve 2 tablespoons of the bean mixture. Layer the
remaining bean mixture over the lettuce. Reserve 1 tablespoon of the tomatoes.
Layer the remaining tomatoes over the bean mixture. Reserve 1 tablespoon of
the corn mixture. Layer the remaining corn mixture over the tomatoes.
Sprinkle with the cheese. Cut the avocado into halves lengthwise, reserving
$^1/_2$ for another purpose. Peel the remaining half and cut into slices. Arrange
over the salad in spoke-like fashion. Fill in the spaces between the avocado
slices alternately with the reserved beans, reserved tomatoes, reserved corn
and bacon. Garnish with a cilantro sprig. Serve with Cilantro Vinaigrette.

Cilantro Vinaigrette

YIELD: 1 CUP

3 to 5 jalapeño chiles, seeded
1/4 cup white wine vinegar
1 garlic clove

1 teaspoon salt
2/3 cup olive oil
1/2 cup packed fresh cilantro

Purée the chiles with the vinegar, garlic and salt. Add the oil in a fine stream, processing constantly. Add the cilantro. Process until finely chopped.

Patti Pine
Vera Bradley Sales Representative Coordinator

Almond Cherry Chicken Salad

YIELD: 10 TO 12 SERVINGS

Traverse City is the cherry capital of the world, and this recipe makes good use of a local product.

9 to 10 cups chopped cooked chicken
2 cups chopped celery
2 cups dried cherries
1 cup sliced almonds, toasted
1 1/2 cups mayonnaise

1/2 cup half-and-half
1/4 cup apple cider vinegar
2 teaspoons salt
1/4 cup grated onion

Combine the chicken, celery, cherries and almonds in a large bowl and toss to mix well. Blend the mayonnaise, half-and-half, vinegar and salt in a bowl. Stir in the onion. Pour over the chicken mixture and toss to mix well. Chill, covered, in the refrigerator. Serve on lettuce-lined salad plates. You may purchase dried cherries by catalog through American Spoon Foods.

Nancy Pishney
Creative Needle Arts, Ltd.
Traverse City, Michigan

Chicken and Corn Tostada Salad

This is the best taco salad—well worth trying for your family.

1 tablespoon olive oil
2 boneless skinless chicken breasts,
   cut into strips
1/2 teaspoon garlic salt
1 (16-ounce) can whole kernel corn,
   drained
1 cup chopped tomatoes
1 (15-ounce) can black beans,
   drained, rinsed
5 green onions with tops, thinly sliced
2 medium avocados, peeled, chopped

1/4 cup cider vinegar
3 tablespoons honey
1 1/2 teaspoons cumin
1/4 teaspoon salt
1/4 teaspoon pepper
1 head Boston or Bibb lettuce,
   torn into bite-size pieces
1 small red bell pepper, chopped
2 cups shredded Monterey Jack cheese
3 cups lightly crushed blue corn
   tortilla chips

Heat the oil in a large skillet over medium-high heat. Add the chicken. Cook for 5 minutes or until cooked through. Remove to a large bowl and sprinkle with the garlic salt. Stir in the corn. Chill, covered, for 30 minutes. Add the tomatoes, beans, green onions and avocados and toss to mix well.

Combine the vinegar, honey, cumin, salt and pepper in a jar with a tight-fitting lid. Cover and shake well. Pour over the chicken mixture and toss to coat well.

To serve, arrange the lettuce and bell pepper on each serving plate. Add the chicken mixture. Top with the cheese and tortilla chips. Garnish with salsa and sour cream.

Dan's Tog Shop
Menomonee Falls, Wisconsin

Curried Chicken Salad

YIELD: 4 SERVINGS

Great when made with grilled chicken, this salad also makes
a nice sandwich served on a croissant.

4 chicken breasts	1/2 cup almonds, toasted
1 cup green grape halves	1/2 cup minced parsley
3/4 cup chopped celery	Curried Mayonnaise (below)

Place the chicken on a grill rack. Grill over hot coals until cooked through.
Let stand until cool. Cut into bite-size pieces.

Combine the chicken, grapes, celery, almonds and parsley in a large bowl.
Add the Curried Mayonnaise and stir until moistened. Serve on lettuce-lined
serving plates.

Curried Mayonnaise

YIELD: 4 SERVINGS

1 cup mayonnaise	2 teaspoons ground ginger
1/3 cup milk	Salt and white pepper to taste
1 tablespoon curry powder	

Blend the mayonnaise, milk, curry powder, ginger, salt and white pepper in a
bowl. Adjust the seasonings to taste.

Allie Carmack
Edinburgh Gardens
Columbus, Ohio

Orange Cashew Chicken Salad

YIELD: 4 TO 6 SERVINGS

4 boneless skinless chicken breasts
3 ribs celery, chopped
1 head romaine, torn into bite-size
   pieces

2 red bell peppers, seeded, julienned
4 green onions, sliced
1 cup salted cashew halves
Sweet-and-Sour Dressing (below)

Place the chicken on a grill rack. Grill over hot coals until cooked through. Cut into 1/4-inch strips and place in a large bowl. Add the celery, romaine, bell peppers, green onions and cashews and toss to mix well. Add enough of the Sweet-and-Sour Dressing to lightly coat or to taste. Chill, covered, for 2 hours or longer to enhance the flavor.

To serve, spoon onto a serving platter. Garnish with fresh orange slices and fresh parsley.

Sweet-and-Sour Dressing

YIELD: ABOUT 2 CUPS

1 cup fresh cilantro
1/2 cup fresh parsley
1/2 cup olive oil
1/2 cup fresh orange juice
1 tablespoon red wine vinegar

1 tablespoon Dijon mustard
4 teaspoons sugar
2 teaspoons Tabasco sauce, or to taste
1 teaspoon salt
Freshly ground pepper to taste

Process the cilantro, parsley, oil, orange juice, vinegar, Dijon mustard, sugar, Tabasco sauce, salt and pepper in a food processor until smooth.

Katie Burns
Friend of Vera Bradley Designs

The orange juice in the dressing gives this salad a delightful, refreshing taste. For a zesty, light summer luncheon, try serving this with a simple, fresh fruit mix of orange, grapefruit, and pineapple and a side of plain yogurt sweetened with honey.

Shrimp and Pasta Salad with Tomatoes and Avocado

YIELD: 4 SERVINGS

This is an excellent summertime brunch entrée served with crusty bread.

1 pound cooked peeled shrimp
8 ounces rotini or bow tie pasta,
    cooked, drained
1 pint red cherry tomatoes,
    cut into halves
3 scallions, sliced 1/4 inch thick

1 yellow bell pepper, seeded, chopped
Cilantro Lime Vinaigrette (below)
Red or green leaf lettuce
1 small avocado, peeled, cut into slices
1/4 cup fresh cilantro

Combine the shrimp, pasta, tomatoes, scallions and bell pepper in a large bowl. Add 3/4 of the Cilantro Lime Vinaigrette and toss to coat.

To serve, arrange the lettuce leaves on individual salad plates. Spoon the shrimp mixture on the prepared plates. Arrange the avocado on the salad, drizzling with the remaining Cilantro Lime Vinaigrette as needed. Sprinkle with the cilantro.

Cilantro Lime Vinaigrette

YIELD: 4 SERVINGS

3 tablespoons fresh lime juice
3 tablespoons white wine vinegar
1 tablespoon finely chopped fresh
    cilantro

1 tablespoon Dijon mustard
1/4 teaspoon salt
Freshly ground pepper to taste

Combine the lime juice, vinegar, cilantro, Dijon mustard, salt and pepper in a jar with a tight-fitting lid. Cover the jar and shake well.

Barbara Bradley Baekgaard
President and Co-Founder of Vera Bradley

Pasta Salad with Basil, Sungold Cherry Tomatoes and Goat Cheese

YIELD: 4 TO 6 SERVINGS

1 teaspoon salt
1 tablespoon olive oil
1 pound dried rotelle or similar pasta
3 tablespoons olive oil
2 cups Sungold or other cherry
    tomato halves

1 cup fresh basil, coarsely chopped
8 ounces soft fresh goat cheese
1 teaspoon salt
1 teaspoon freshly ground pepper

Bring a large saucepan filled with water to a boil. Add 1 teaspoon salt and 1 tablespoon oil. Add the pasta. Cook for 7 to 10 minutes or until al dente, stirring occasionally. Drain in a colander and rinse under cold running water.

Place the pasta in a large serving bowl. Add 3 tablespoons oil, tomatoes and basil. Crumble the goat cheese over the top and toss to mix well. Sprinkle with 1 teaspoon salt and pepper. Serve at room temperature.

Amy Grinsfelder
Vera Bradley Marketing Design Coordinator

Fresh Spring Asparagus

YIELD: 8 SERVINGS

2 to 3 pounds fresh asparagus
Juice of 1 lemon

Salt and pepper to taste

Trim the asparagus. Place in a large skillet and add enough water to cover. Cover and bring to a boil. Cook for 3 to 6 minutes or until tender-crisp. Remove with tongs to a serving platter. Sprinkle with the lemon juice. Season with salt and pepper.

Sue Britton
Vera Bradley Marketing Manager

86   Soups, Salads & Sides

Wild Mushroom Bread Pudding

YIELD: 6 SERVINGS

This recipe was inspired by a wonderful memory I have of mushroom hunting with my two sisters and brother in our family's woods.

3 tablespoons olive oil
6 ounces shiitake mushrooms, stems removed, thickly sliced
6 ounces button mushrooms, stems removed, thickly sliced
6 ounces cremini mushrooms, stems removed, thickly sliced
2 portobello mushroom caps, thinly sliced
4 teaspoons chopped garlic
1/4 cup dry red wine
1 tablespoon chopped fresh basil

1 tablespoon chopped fresh parsley
1 teaspoon dried sage
1 teaspoon dried thyme
Salt and pepper to taste
5 eggs
2 cups heavy cream
1 cup milk
1/4 cup grated Parmesan cheese
3/4 teaspoon salt
1/2 teaspoon pepper
6 cups trimmed French bread cubes
2 tablespoons grated Parmesan cheese

Heat the oil in a large heavy stockpot over medium-high heat. Add the mushrooms, garlic, wine, basil, parsley, sage and thyme. Sauté for 15 minutes or until the mushrooms are tender. Remove from heat. Season with salt and pepper to taste.

Whisk the eggs, cream, milk, 1/4 cup Parmesan cheese, 3/4 teaspoon salt and 1/2 teaspoon pepper in a large bowl. Add the bread cubes and toss to coat. Let stand for 15 minutes. Stir in the sautéed mushroom mixture. Spoon into an 8×8-inch glass baking dish sprayed with nonstick cooking spray. Sprinkle with 2 tablespoons Parmesan cheese. Bake at 350 degrees for 1 hour or until brown, puffed and set in the center. Serve warm.

Cheri Lantz
Vera Bradley Sales Analyst

Creamy Mushroom Bake

YIELD: 8 SERVINGS

Use a variety of mushrooms, such as cremini, shiitake or
portobello, for an even better version.

1 pound mushrooms, stems removed	1/4 cup vegetable stock
1/2 cup (1 stick) butter	1/2 cup fresh bread crumbs
2 tablespoons flour	1/2 cup grated Parmesan cheese
1/2 cup half-and-half	

Arrange the mushrooms in a buttered 1-quart baking dish. Melt the butter in
a saucepan over low heat. Increase heat to medium. Whisk in the flour. Cook
for 3 minutes. Whisk in the half-and-half and stock. Bring to a boil. Cook until
thickened, stirring constantly. Pour over the mushrooms. Sprinkle with the
bread crumbs. Bake at 350 degrees for 30 minutes. Sprinkle with the Parmesan
cheese. Bake for 5 minutes.

Vi MacMurdo
Lady Vi
Volant, Pennsylvania

Baked Vidalia Onions

YIELD: 4 SERVINGS

These onions are a great accompaniment to grilled steaks or pork chops.

4 medium to large Vidalia onions	1/2 cup grated Parmesan cheese
1/4 cup (1/2 stick) butter or margarine	Salt and pepper to taste
4 beef or chicken bouillon cubes	

Cut each onion into quarters, cutting to but not through the bottom. Place
1/4 tablespoon butter on each quarter and 1 bouillon cube in the center of
each onion. Sprinkle with Parmesan cheese, salt and pepper. Wrap each
onion individually in foil. Bake at 400 degrees for 1 hour. Unwrap the onions
and serve immediately.

Nancy Graham
Vera Bradley Customer Service—Retired

Cheesy Onion Casserole

A great side dish that really goes with everything.

3 medium onions, thinly sliced
1/4 cup (1/2 stick) butter
1/2 green bell pepper, chopped
2 tablespoons chopped pimentos
1 cup shredded Swiss cheese

1 cup cracker crumbs
2 eggs, beaten
3/4 cup half-and-half
1 teaspoon salt
1/2 teaspoon pepper

Sauté the onions in the butter in a medium skillet for 7 minutes or until tender. Add the bell pepper. Sauté for 4 minutes. Remove from heat. Stir in the pimentos.

Layer the onion mixture, cheese and cracker crumbs 1/2 at a time in a medium baking dish. Whisk the eggs, half-and-half, salt and pepper in a bowl. Pour over the top. Bake at 325 degrees for 25 minutes.

Jeannine Wallace
Shop of the Gulls
Charlevoix, Michigan

Easy Cheesy Spuds

This is a great, easy way of doing scalloped potatoes—and it really works.

3 tablespoons butter
4 medium potatoes, sliced
   1/8 inch thick
1 cup Cheddar cheese
1/2 cup thinly sliced onion

1 teaspoon salt
1/4 teaspoon pepper
1 cup milk
1 tablespoon flour

Spread 1 tablespoon of the butter in a 12-inch skillet. Layer the potatoes, cheese, onion, remaining butter, salt and pepper 1/2 at a time in the prepared skillet. Blend the milk and flour in a bowl. Pour over the layers. Bring to a simmer over high heat. Reduce heat to medium-low. Cook, covered, for 25 minutes or until the potatoes are tender. Simmer, uncovered, for 7 minutes or until the sauce thickens.

Lyn Killoran
Friend of Vera Bradley

Garlic Mashed Red Potatoes

YIELD: 4 SERVINGS

3 unpeeled new red potatoes,
   quartered
1 tablespoon olive oil
1 garlic clove, minced
1/4 cup sour cream

1/4 cup (about) milk, at room
   temperature
2 teaspoons cider vinegar, or to taste
Salt and freshly ground pepper to taste

Place the potatoes with cold water to cover in a medium saucepan. Bring to a boil and reduce heat. Simmer for 20 minutes or until tender; drain. Return to the saucepan and cover with a lid.

Heat the olive oil in a small skillet over medium heat. Add the garlic. Sauté for 2 minutes. Beat the potatoes and garlic in a mixing bowl until mashed. Add the sour cream. Beat at medium-high speed until smooth. Add the milk gradually until of the desired consistency, beating constantly. Beat in the vinegar. Season with salt and pepper. Serve immediately.

Emilie Robertson
Vera Bradley Customer Service

Chip's Grilled Potatoes

YIELD: 6 SERVINGS

My husband cooks these potatoes quite a bit in the summer. They are delicious and there is no mess to clean up afterward.

6 medium potatoes, chopped
1 medium onion, chopped
2 ribs celery, chopped
2 slices bacon, chopped

1/2 cup olive oil
2 tablespoons cornstarch
Rosemary, thyme, salt and pepper
   to taste

Combine the potatoes, onion, celery and bacon in a medium bowl and toss to mix well. Place on a large piece of foil coated with nonstick cooking spray.

Whisk the oil, cornstarch, rosemary, thyme, salt and pepper in a 2-cup glass measure. Drizzle over the potato mixture. Top with another piece of foil sprayed with nonstick cooking spray. Seal the edges to form a pocket. Place on a grill rack. Grill over hot coals for 1 hour. The potatoes will cook evenly so there is no need to turn over the packet.

Stefanie Chevillet
Vera Bradley Customer Service

Shredded Parmesan Potatoes

....

YIELD: 8 SERVINGS

8 medium potatoes
2 bunches green onions with tops,
    sliced
1/2 cup grated Parmesan cheese
2 teaspoons salt

2 teaspoons pepper
1/4 cup (1/2 stick) butter,
    cut into pats
Paprika to taste

Place the potatoes in a large stockpot with water to cover. Boil for 20 minutes or until tender; drain. Cool slightly. Peel the potatoes. Shred with a knife or in a food processor. Place in a large mixing bowl. Add the green onions. Stir in the Parmesan cheese, salt and pepper. Spoon into a large baking dish coated with nonstick cooking spray. Dot with butter randomly over the top. Sprinkle with paprika. Bake at 350 degrees for 40 minutes or until the top begins to brown. Let stand for 10 minutes before serving.

Patricia R. Miller
President and Co-Founder of Vera Bradley

Make-Ahead Mashed Potatoes

....

YIELD: 8 SERVINGS

Perfect for Thanksgiving dinner when you have a thousand things on
the stove. Just make ahead, pull out of the refrigerator and bake.

5 pounds potatoes, peeled, quartered
6 ounces cream cheese, softened
1 cup sour cream
2 tablespoons butter or margarine

2 teaspoons onion salt
1 teaspoon salt
1/4 teaspoon pepper

Cook the potatoes in boiling water to cover in a saucepan until tender; drain well. Mash until smooth. Add the cream cheese, sour cream, 2 tablespoons butter, onion salt, salt and pepper and beat until smooth and fluffy. Spoon into a buttered 9×13-inch baking dish. Dot with additional butter. Bake at 350 degrees for 30 minutes or until heated through.

Kim Colby
Vera Bradley Vice President of Design

Twice-Baked Potatoes

4 medium potatoes
3 tablespoons butter
1/4 cup sour cream
2 ounces cream cheese
1/4 cup grated Parmesan cheese

2/3 cup milk
1 teaspoon salt
1 teaspoon chives
1/2 teaspoon pepper
1/2 cup shredded Cheddar cheese

Scrub the potatoes and pierce with a fork. Bake at 350 degrees for 1 hour or until tender. Cut the top off the potatoes lengthwise. Scoop the pulp into a mixing bowl, reserving the shells. Add the butter, sour cream, cream cheese, Parmesan cheese, milk, salt, chives and pepper and beat well. Add additional milk if needed for the desired consistency. Spoon into the reserved shells. Sprinkle with the Cheddar cheese. Place on a baking sheet. Bake at 350 degrees for 10 minutes or until the cheese melts.

Helen Bigg
Vera Bradley Sales Representative

Our **Return to Happiness** *fabric is one of our favorites because of its wonderfully fresh quality and its very touching message.*

"Courage, Compassion, Commitment" . . . for us, these are the words that define the fight against breast cancer. After losing a dear friend to this disease, Vera Bradley co-owners, Barbara Baekgaard and Patricia Miller, founded the Vera Bradley Classic. Since 1994, this annual women's golf and tennis competition has raised over $1 million for breast cancer research and programs. In addition, the Vera Bradley Foundation for Breast Cancer was established in 1998 and has pledged $1.2 million to endow a chair in oncology at the Indiana University School of Medicine in Indianapolis. Net proceeds go directly to this commitment.

In support of the Foundation, we designed this **Return to Happiness** *fabric. Pink ribbons symbolize breast cancer awareness, while dainty lilies of the valley traditionally stand for a "return to happiness."*

Sautéed Spinach with Mushrooms

YIELD: 4 TO 6 SERVINGS

Grandma always said, "Eat your spinach!" Try this as a tasty variation.

2 pounds fresh spinach, trimmed
2 tablespoons olive oil
1 medium onion, finely chopped
1 garlic clove, minced
1 cup sliced fresh mushrooms

2 teaspoons lemon juice
1 teaspoon salt
3/4 teaspoon sugar
Freshly ground pepper to taste

Tear the spinach into bite-size pieces. Heat the oil in a large skillet over medium-high heat. Add the onion. Sauté for 5 minutes or until tender. Stir in the garlic and mushrooms. Cook for 2 minutes. Stir in the spinach, lemon juice, salt, sugar and pepper. Cook, covered, for 10 minutes, stirring occasionally.

Patti Reedy
Vera Bradley Sales Representative
Granddaughter of Vera Bradley

Brandied Sweet Potatoes

YIELD: 6 TO 8 SERVINGS

Ok, this is what *really* got Bill . . . (see page 65)!

5 large sweet potatoes (about 4 1/2
   pounds)
1/4 cup sugar
1/4 to 1/3 cup brandy
3 tablespoons butter or margarine,
   melted
1 teaspoon salt

1/2 teaspoon nutmeg
1/2 teaspoon ginger
1/8 teaspoon pepper
1 tablespoon butter or margarine,
   melted
1 tablespoon orange zest
1 cup ground pecans

Cook the sweet potatoes in boiling water to cover in a large stockpot for 45 minutes or until tender; drain. Cool slightly. Peel the sweet potatoes and place in a large mixing bowl. Beat the sweet potatoes until mashed. Add the sugar, brandy, 3 tablespoons butter, salt, nutmeg, ginger and pepper and beat well. Spoon into a lightly greased 7×11-inch baking dish. Brush with 1 tablespoon melted butter. Sprinkle with the orange zest and pecans. Bake at 350 degrees for 25 to 30 minutes or until heated through. Garnish with orange slices.

Debra Bleeke
Vera Bradley Customer Service

Tomato and Green Bean Risotto with Feta Cheese

YIELD: 6 TO 8 SERVINGS

The first time I made this recipe, I gathered all the ingredients except the tomatoes . . . . Luckily, my neighbor had some growing in a pot *on her roof!*

8 sun-dried tomatoes
1 (14-ounce) can French-cut
  green beans
2/3 cup dry white wine
3 (10-ounce) cans chicken broth
2 teaspoons olive oil
1 cup chopped onion

2 garlic cloves, minced
1 1/2 cups uncooked short grain
  white rice
1 teaspoon basil
1/8 teaspoon salt
3/4 cup crumbled feta cheese

Soak the sun-dried tomatoes in hot water to cover in a bowl until soft; drain. Cut into thin strips.

Drain the beans, reserving the liquid. Mix the reserved liquid with the wine and broth in a bowl.

Heat the oil in a large skillet over medium heat. Add the onion and garlic. Sauté for 3 minutes. Add the rice. Cook for 1 minute, stirring constantly. Add the broth mixture 1 cup at a time, stirring constantly until each portion of the broth mixture is absorbed; this will take about 20 minutes. Add the tomatoes, green beans, basil and salt. Cook for 2 minutes, stirring constantly. Remove from heat. Stir in the cheese. Serve immediately.

Stefanie Chevillet
Vera Bradley Customer Service

Roasted Tomato and Garlic Sauce

YIELD: ABOUT 2 CUPS

6 Roma or plum tomatoes
6 garlic cloves, peeled
2 tablespoons olive oil
1/4 cup balsamic vinegar
2/3 cup olive oil

2 tablespoons water
2 tablespoons sugar
1 tablespoon basil
1 teaspoon oregano
1 tablespoon parsley flakes

Layer the tomatoes and garlic in a small baking dish. Drizzle with 2 tablespoons olive oil. Bake at 350 degrees until roasted, turning once.

Combine the roasted tomatoes, garlic, balsamic vinegar, 2/3 cup olive oil, water, sugar, basil, oregano and parsley flakes in a blender container and process until blended. Serve over steamed fresh green beans or vegetables.

Jolene Doyle
G. B. Heron's Clothiers & Tailors
Rice Lake, Wisconsin

Cold Sun-Dried Tomato and Feta Soufflé

YIELD: 6 servings

This can be prepared up to four days in advance and refrigerated,
or it can be frozen for up to three months.

2 envelopes unflavored gelatin
1/4 cup madeira or dry red wine
2 cups (or more) sun-dried tomatoes, minced
1/2 to 3/4 cup feta cheese
2 cups sour cream
2 cups cream cheese

1/2 cup parsley, minced
2 to 4 shallots
3 to 4 garlic cloves
1/4 to 1/2 cup marinated red peppers or pimentos
2 tablespoons dillweed or rosemary
Salt and white pepper to taste

Dissolve the gelatin in 2 tablespoons of the wine in a small bowl set in a larger bowl of hot water. Combine the gelatin mixture, remaining wine, 1/2 of the tomatoes, feta cheese, sour cream, cream cheese, parsley, shallots, garlic cloves, marinated red peppers, dillweed, salt and white pepper in a food processor container fitted with a steel blade. Process until blended. Adjust seasonings to taste. Stir in the remaining tomatoes gently. Pour into an oiled 6-cup soufflé dish. Chill for 4 hours or until firm.

To serve, run a knife around the edge of the mold, dipping the bottom of the mold in warm water to loosen if needed. Invert onto a serving plate.

Mary Ann Gray
Vera Bradley Sales Representative

Connoisseur's Casserole

YIELD: 8 SERVINGS

A great side dish served with any pork or beef entrée.

1 (12-ounce) can whole kernel corn,
  drained
1 (16-ounce) can French-cut
  green beans, drained
1/2 cup chopped celery
1/2 cup chopped onion
1 (2-ounce) jar chopped pimentos
1 (10-ounce) can cream of
  mushroom soup

1/2 cup sour cream
1/2 cup shredded sharp Cheddar cheese
Salt and pepper to taste
1 cup butter cracker crumbs
1/4 cup (1/2 stick) butter or margarine,
  melted
1/2 cup slivered almonds

Combine the corn, green beans, celery, onion, pimentos, soup, sour cream, cheese, salt and pepper in a large bowl and mix well. Spoon into a greased 1 1/2-quart baking dish. Mix the cracker crumbs, butter and almonds in a bowl. Sprinkle over the top. Bake at 350 degrees for 45 minutes.

Susie Bruce
Vera Bradley Merchandising Coordinator—Retired

Southern Succotash

YIELD: 8 SERVINGS

The okra makes this a truly southern dish.

1 tablespoon olive oil
1 garlic clove, minced
1 onion, minced
1 red bell pepper, chopped
Salt and pepper to taste
1/4 teaspoon ginger

1 (10-ounce) package frozen corn
1 (10-ounce) package frozen baby
  lima beans
1/2 cup fresh okra, trimmed, sliced
1 1/4 cups water

Heat the oil in a large skillet over medium heat. Add the garlic, onion and bell pepper. Sauté until tender. Season with salt and pepper. Add the ginger, corn, lima beans, okra and water. Simmer, covered, for 8 minutes. Simmer, uncovered, for 5 minutes longer or until most of the liquid is evaporated.

Dorothy McAfee
Cynthia's at Palatka Office Supply
Palatka, Florida

Southwestern-Style Corn Bread Dressing

YIELD: 8 SERVINGS

This is a delicious southern dressing perfect at
Thanksgiving for a little different taste.

2 (8-ounce) packages corn bread mix
2 to 3 teaspoons cumin seeds
1/4 cup (1/2 stick) butter or margarine
2 cups finely chopped celery
1/2 cup chopped onion
1/2 cup chopped red bell pepper
1/2 cup chopped green bell pepper
1 (8-ounce) package herb-seasoned
  stuffing mix

2 (10-ounce) cans reduced-sodium
  chicken broth
21/4 cups water
2 eggs, lightly beaten
1/2 teaspoon salt
1/2 teaspoon red pepper

Prepare the corn bread mix using the package directions. Let stand until cool.
Crumble into a large bowl.

Sauté the cumin seeds in a small nonstick skillet over medium heat for
3 minutes or until fragrant and light brown. Let stand until cool. Crush the
cumin seeds.

Melt the butter in a skillet over medium heat. Add the celery, onion and
bell peppers. Sauté until tender. Stir into the crumbled corn bread. Add the
crushed cumin, stuffing mix, broth, water, eggs, salt and red pepper and mix
well. Spoon into a greased 9×13-inch baking dish. Bake at 350 degrees for
11/4 hours or until light brown.

Katie Burns
Friend of Vera Bradley Designs

Zucchini Gratin with Parmesan Cheese and Thyme

YIELD: 8 SERVINGS

2 tablespoons olive oil
2 medium onions, thinly sliced
2 garlic cloves, minced (optional)
1 1/4 pounds tomatoes, cut into slices
   1/4 inch thick
2 small zucchini, cut diagonally
   1/4 inch thick
2 small yellow squash, cut diagonally
   1/4 inch thick
1 1/2 tablespoons olive oil

2 tablespoons fresh thyme leaves
1/2 teaspoon coarse salt
1 1/4 cups freshly grated Parmesan
   cheese or Gruyère cheese
1 tablespoon fresh thyme leaves
Freshly ground pepper to taste
1/2 teaspoon coarse salt
1 1/2 tablespoons olive oil
1 tablespoon fresh thyme leaves

Heat 2 tablespoons oil in a medium skillet over medium heat. Add the onions. Sauté for 20 minutes or until transparent and golden brown, reducing heat to medium-low if browning too quickly. Add the garlic. Sauté until fragrant. Spread evenly in a greased oval baking dish. Let cool.

Place the tomatoes on a shallow plate. Let stand for a few minutes; drain. Toss the zucchini and yellow squash with 1 1/2 tablespoons oil, 2 tablespoons thyme and 1/2 teaspoon salt in a bowl. Reserve 1/2 of the cheese for the topping.

Sprinkle 1 tablespoon thyme over the onion layer. Arrange a row of slightly overlapping tomato slices across the width of the prepared dish, beginning at one end. Sprinkle with some of the remaining cheese. Arrange a row of zucchini overlapping the tomato slices by 2/3. Sprinkle with some of the remaining cheese. Arrange a row of yellow squash overlapping the zucchini by 2/3. Sprinkle with some of the remaining cheese. Repeat rows until the baking dish is full, sprinkling each row with cheese. Season lightly with pepper and 1/2 teaspoon salt. Drizzle 1 1/2 tablespoons oil over the layers. Mix the reserved cheese with 1 tablespoon thyme. Sprinkle over the top. Bake at 375 degrees for 65 to 70 minutes or until brown and bubbly. Cool for 15 minutes or longer before serving.

Dede Hall
Vera Bradley Classic Volunteer

Cranberry Sauce with Apricots and Raisins

4 cups fresh cranberries
1 cup dried apricots, chopped
1 cup golden raisins
3/4 cup sugar

1 cup water
1 cup orange juice
1 tablespoon orange zest

Combine the cranberries, apricots, raisins, sugar, water, orange juice and orange zest in a heavy saucepan. Cook over medium heat until the sugar dissolves, stirring constantly. Increase the heat to medium-high. Cover and bring to a boil. Boil for 8 minutes or until the cranberries pop, stirring occasionally. Spoon into a serving bowl. Chill, covered, in the refrigerator. The sauce will thicken as it chills. You may prepare the sauce up to 4 days in advance.

Mary Beth Wahl
Vera Bradley Marketing Director—Retired

DINNER IS SERVED
ENTRÉES

Beef with Shrimp

YIELD: 2 SERVINGS

2 tablespoons flour
Salt and freshly ground pepper to taste
2 (4-ounce) beef fillets, trimmed
2 tablespoons butter
1 bunch green onions, finely chopped
2 teaspoons finely chopped chives
1/2 teaspoon dried dillweed
1/4 cup dry red wine

1/2 cup beef stock
2 tablespoons butter
4 cherry tomatoes, quartered
1 teaspoon lemon juice
4 large shrimp, peeled, deveined, butterflied
1 tablespoon parsley
4 lemon peel shreds

Mix the flour with salt and pepper in a shallow dish. Dredge the beef in the flour mixture, shaking off the excess. Heat 2 tablespoons butter in a large skillet over medium-high heat; do not allow the butter to brown. Add the beef. Cook for 3 minutes on each side for medium-rare or to the desired degree of doneness. Remove to a warm platter and tent with foil to keep warm.

Sauté the green onions, chives and dillweed in the drippings in the skillet until brown. Add the wine. Cook until almost all the liquid is evaporated, stirring constantly. Add the beef stock. Simmer until the mixture is reduced by half. Whisk in 2 tablespoons butter. Add the tomatoes, lemon juice and shrimp. Cook for 2 minutes or until the shrimp turn pink. Arrange 1 beef fillet on each individual serving plate. Top with 2 shrimp opened over the beef. Spoon 3 tablespoons of the sauce over the top. Sprinkle with the parsley and lemon peel.

Jill Nichols
Vera Bradley Executive Vice President/COO

Marinated Flank Steak

YIELD: 4 SERVINGS

This is the first thing that my husband Butch and
I grill when spring finally arrives.

1 cup chablis or other dry white wine
1/4 cup soy sauce
1 envelope meat marinade
2 tablespoons olive oil

1 tablespoon sugar
2 garlic cloves, crushed
1 (2-pound) flank steak

Combine the wine, soy sauce, meat marinade, oil, sugar and garlic in a shallow
dish and mix well. Add the steak. Marinate, covered, in the refrigerator for
3 hours or longer, turning the steak occasionally; drain. Place the steak on a
grill rack. Grill for 7 minutes on each side or to the desired degree of doneness.
To serve, slice steak thinly across the grain.

Patti Pine
Vera Bradley Sales Representative Coordinator

Tabasco Seared Rib-Eye Steaks

YIELD: 6 SERVINGS

3 (1-pound) rib-eye steaks, about
   1 1/2 inches thick

Tabasco sauce
2 teaspoons cracked pepper

Place the steaks on a cutting board. Trim any excess fat from each steak.
Place the steaks on a large plate. Rub 3 dashes Tabasco sauce into each steak.
Sprinkle each steak with 1/3 teaspoon pepper and rub into each. Repeat on
the other side of the steaks. Place on a grill rack over medium heat. Grill for
8 to 10 minutes or to the desired degree of doneness, turning halfway through
grilling time. Remove from the grill and let stand for 5 minutes. Cut each steak
diagonally into thin strips. Serve immediately.

Mike Ray
Vera Bradley Vice President of Sales

Forgotten Roast

This dish is perfect when: 1) You don't know what time dinner will be; 2) You'd rather be playing 18 holes of golf; or 3) You're working all day and entertaining that night. The secret is to keep the oven CLOSED at all times. We've found that posting a sign on the oven door is very helpful, since the aroma tempts people to open it for a "peak"!

1 standing rib roast (any size)	Pepper
Seasoned salt	8 potatoes, parboiled

Place the roast on a rack in a roasting pan. Sprinkle generously with seasonings. Place in a 400-degree oven. Roast for 1 hour. Turn off the oven and let the roast remain in the oven all day. DO NOT OPEN THE OVEN DOOR! A half-hour before we are ready to eat, I often parboil the potatoes and place them in the roasting pan with the roast. Then I simply turn the oven back on to 400 degrees and bake for 30 minutes for medium-rare, or 45 minutes for medium. So good, so easy and so juicy!

Barbara Bradley Baekgaard
President and Co-Founder of Vera Bradley

Braised Beef

YIELD: 4 SERVINGS

Best made the day before and reheated.

2 pounds stewing beef, cubed	1 1/2 to 4 tablespoons flour
1 pound fresh mushrooms	2 tablespoons parsley
1/4 cup (1/2 stick) butter	1 teaspoon oregano
3 (8-ounce) cans tomato sauce	2 teaspoons seasoned salt
1 cup plus 2 tablespoons burgundy or other dry red wine	Salt and pepper to taste

Sauté the beef and mushrooms in the butter in a skillet. Stir in the tomato sauce and wine. Add enough flour to make of the desired consistency, stirring constantly. Mixture will be slightly runny. Stir in the parsley, oregano, seasoned salt, salt and pepper. Spoon into a large baking dish. Bake at 325 degrees for 2 1/2 hours. Serve over hot cooked rice.

Joyce Neubauer
Vera Bradley Classic Steering Committee

Classic Beef Stew

YIELD: 8 SERVINGS

I used to make this in the fall when I first moved to Florida. Although October in Tampa can still be sweltering, we'd turn up the air conditioner, put on sweaters, light a fire in the fireplace and have a bowl of stew.

8 ounces bacon, finely chopped
3 pounds boneless beef chuck,
    trimmed, cut into 1¹/₂-inch pieces
Salt and pepper to taste
¹/₃ cup flour
1¹/₄ pounds small boiling onions
12 ounces carrots, cut into
    1-inch pieces
12 large garlic cloves

3 cups canned beef broth
¹/₂ cup Cognac or other brandy
2 (750-milliliter) bottles red burgundy
1¹/₄ pounds button mushrooms
2 tablespoons thyme
2 bay leaves
1 tablespoon brown sugar
1 tablespoon tomato paste

Cook the bacon in a Dutch oven until crisp. Remove the bacon with a slotted spoon to paper towels to drain. Season the beef generously with salt and pepper. Dredge in the flour, shaking off the excess. Place in the bacon drippings. Brown over high heat for 5 minutes, stirring constantly. Remove to a large bowl. Crumble the bacon over the beef. Sauté the onions and carrots in the pan drippings for 6 minutes or until brown. Add the garlic. Sauté for 1 minute. Remove the vegetables to the bowl with the beef.

Add 1 cup of the beef broth and the Cognac to the pan drippings. Boil for 8 minutes or until of a glaze consistency, stirring to deglaze the Dutch oven. Return the undrained beef and vegetables to the Dutch oven. Add the wine, mushrooms, thyme, bay leaves, brown sugar, tomato paste and remaining 2 cups beef broth. Bring to a boil, stirring occasionally. Cover the Dutch oven. Bake at 350 degrees for 1¹/₂ hours or until the beef is tender. Skim the top. Season with salt and pepper. Discard the bay leaves before serving.

Michael Nelaborige
Vera Bradley Marketing Assistant

Chile Relleno Casserole

This is a great casserole to take along for potluck dinners. It is even better the next day and can be easily microwaved to reheat.

1 large onion, finely chopped	3 eggs
2 tablespoons olive oil	3 cups milk
1 1/2 pounds ground beef	3/4 cup flour
27 ounces canned whole green chiles	1 1/2 teaspoons salt
2 pounds Monterey Jack cheese, sliced	1 (16-ounce) jar salsa
	1 pound Cheddar cheese, grated

Brown the onion in the olive oil in a skillet until transparent. Add the ground beef. Cook until brown, stirring until crumbly; drain.

Cut the chiles vertically and remove the seeds. Open the chiles and lay enough in the bottom of a large baking dish to cover. Layer 1/2 of the Monterey Jack cheese, ground beef mixture, remaining Monterey Jack cheese and remaining chiles in the prepared dish. Beat the eggs, milk, flour and salt in a bowl until blended. Pour over the layers.

Bake at 350 degrees for 45 minutes or until set. Pour the salsa over the top. Sprinkle with the Cheddar cheese. Broil until bubbly. Let stand for 15 minutes before serving.

Nancy Pishney
Creative Needle Arts, Ltd.
Traverse City, Michigan

Mexican Meat Loaf

....

YIELD: 3 LOAVES

Place a foil-wrapped frozen meat loaf and baking potatoes in a
300-degree oven, go out and play nine holes of golf and—voila—meat loaf
and baked potatoes when you come in.

1 pound ground veal	1/4 cup chopped green bell pepper
1 pound ground pork	1/2 cup chopped celery
1 pound ground beef	1/2 cup chopped onion
2 eggs	1/2 cup chopped green olives
1 (8-ounce) jar taco sauce	1 1/2 cups seasoned bread crumbs

Combine the veal, pork, ground beef, eggs, taco sauce, bell pepper, celery,
onion, olives and bread crumbs in a large bowl and mix well. Shape into
3 loaves. Place in a 9×13-inch glass baking dish. Bake at 350 degrees for
1 1/4 hours or until brown and cooked through.

You may eat 1 loaf and wrap the remaining loaves in foil and freeze for a
quick dinner on a busy day.

Lou Alexander
Legend Lake Golf Club
Chardon, Ohio

Stuffed Leg of Lamb

This has become a family favorite—with repeated requests for it every Easter.

1/4 cup fresh cilantro, chopped
1/4 cup fresh basil
6 garlic cloves, chopped
1/2 tablespoon thyme
1/2 tablespoon rosemary
1 (10-ounce) package frozen chopped
   spinach, thawed
16 ounces ricotta cheese

1 cup chopped walnuts
1 (3- to 4-pound) boned and
   butterflied leg of lamb, trimmed
1/4 cup olive oil
8 ounces Dijon mustard
1/2 cup bread crumbs
Brown Sauce (below)

Mix the cilantro, basil, garlic, thyme and rosemary in a bowl. Squeeze the excess moisture from the spinach. Combine the spinach, cheese and walnuts in a bowl and mix well.

Lay the lamb open like a book on a clean countertop. Rub with the oil. Rub with the cilantro mixture. Spread with the spinach mixture. Roll up beginning at the long end; tie with kitchen string. Cover with the Dijon mustard. Sprinkle with the bread crumbs. Place on a grill rack. Grill over medium heat for 45 minutes or until a thermometer inserted in the thickest portion registers 150 degrees for medium-rare. Serve with Brown Sauce. You may roast at 400 degrees for 50 to 60 minutes or until a thermometer inserted in the thickest portion registers 150 degrees for medium-rare.

Brown Sauce

1 (46-ounce) can beef broth
1 (6-ounce) can tomato paste
1 yellow onion, cut into halves
1/2 tablespoon rosemary
4 bay leaves

3 garlic cloves, crushed
1 1/2 cups red wine
1/2 cup cornstarch
1/2 cup red wine

Combine the broth, tomato paste, onion, rosemary, bay leaves, garlic and 1 1/2 cups wine in a medium saucepan. Bring to a boil and reduce heat. Simmer for 30 minutes. Whisk the cornstarch and 1/2 cup wine in a small bowl until blended. Stir into the broth mixture. Cook until thickened, stirring constantly. Remove the onion and bay leaves with a slotted spoon. Cool for 15 minutes before serving.

Lyn Killoran
Friend of Vera Bradley

Grilled Garlic Lime Pork Tenderloin

YIELD: 4 SERVINGS

A great entrée to serve for a dinner party. The presentation
is beautiful and it is so easy.

6 large garlic cloves, chopped
2 tablespoons soy sauce
2 tablespoons grated fresh gingerroot
2 teaspoons Dijon mustard
1/3 cup fresh lime juice

1/2 cup olive oil
Cayenne pepper to taste
Salt and black pepper to taste
4 (3/4-pound) pork tenderloins
Onion Jalapeño Marmalade (below)

Process the garlic, soy sauce, gingerroot, Dijon mustard, lime juice, oil, cayenne pepper, salt and black pepper in a blender or food processor until blended. Place the pork in a large sealable food storage bag. Pour the marinade over the pork and seal the bag. Place in a shallow dish. Marinate in the refrigerator for 24 hours or longer, turning occasionally.

Let pork stand at room temperature for 30 minutes before grilling. Drain the pork, discarding the marinade. Place on an oiled grill rack. Grill 5 to 6 inches above glowing coals for 15 to 20 minutes or until cooked through, turning every 5 minutes. Remove the pork to a cutting board. Let stand for 5 minutes. Cut into slices. Serve with Onion Jalapeño Marmalade.

Onion Jalapeño Marmalade

YIELD: 4 SERVINGS

1 1/4 pounds red or yellow onions,
    thinly sliced, separated into rings
3 tablespoons olive oil
Salt and pepper to taste

2 fresh jalapeño chiles, seeded, minced
2 tablespoons honey or sugar
3 to 4 tablespoons red wine vinegar
1/4 cup water

Sauté the onions in the oil in a large heavy saucepan over medium heat until softened. Season with salt and pepper to taste. Add the chiles. Sauté for 1 minute. Add the honey. Cook for 1 minute. Add the vinegar. Simmer until almost all of the liquid is evaporated, stirring constantly. Add the water. Simmer for 10 minutes or until slightly thickened, stirring constantly. Season with salt and pepper. You may prepare up to 2 days ahead, store, covered, in the refrigerator and reheat before serving.

Lyn Killoran
Friend of Vera Bradley

Pork Medallions in Creamy Mustard Sauce

YIELD: 4 SERVINGS

1 (1- to 1¹/2-pound) pork tenderloin
¹/2 cup flour
1 teaspoon salt
³/4 teaspoon pepper
3 tablespoons unsalted butter

3 to 6 green onions
¹/3 cup dry white wine
1 cup heavy cream
¹/4 cup Dijon mustard

Cut the pork crosswise into ¹/2-inch slices. Combine the flour, ³/4 teaspoon of the salt and ¹/2 teaspoon of the pepper in a sealable plastic food storage bag and shake to mix well. Add the pork in batches, shaking to coat.

Melt 1 tablespoon of the butter in a large skillet over medium-high heat. Add ¹/3 of the pork. Sauté for 4 to 5 minutes per side or until cooked through. Remove to a platter to keep warm. Repeat the process twice with the remaining pork and 2 tablespoons butter.

Add the green onions to the skillet. Sauté for 1 minute or until tender. Stir in the wine. Bring to a boil. Boil for 3 minutes or until the liquid is reduced to 2 tablespoons. Whisk in the cream. Simmer until thickened, whisking constantly. Whisk in the Dijon mustard. Return the pork to the skillet. Cook until heated through. Sprinkle with ¹/4 teaspoon salt and ¹/4 teaspoon pepper.

Amy Grinsfelder
Vera Bradley Marketing Design Coordinator

Vera's Glazed Pork Roast

YIELD: 8 SERVINGS

This was one of Vera's favorites. She lovingly passed it down to two generations and it is still enjoyed by all!

1 rolled boneless pork roast or
   tenderloin
1 teaspoon chili powder
¹/2 teaspoon garlic powder

¹/2 teaspoon salt
1 cup ketchup
1 cup apple jelly
2 tablespoons vinegar

Rub the pork with a mixture of the chili powder, garlic powder and salt. Place the pork on a rack in a roasting pan. Place in a 450-degree oven. Reduce the oven temperature to 250 degrees. Roast for 40 to 45 minutes per pound or until a meat thermometer inserted in the thickest portion registers 185 degrees.

Whisk the ketchup, jelly and vinegar in a saucepan. Baste the pork with the sauce 15 minutes before the pork is cooked through. Bring the remaining sauce to a boil. Boil for 2 to 3 minutes, stirring constantly. Serve with the pork.

Vera Bradley

Pork Crown Roast with Gravy

YIELD: 6 TO 8 SERVINGS

My mother always made a crown roast for the holidays instead of the usual meats. After she was gone, I wanted the tradition to continue in our family, so this recipe was reinstated at Christmastime.

2 tablespoons olive oil
4 teaspoons thyme
4 teaspoons ground allspice
2 teaspoons salt
1 teaspoon pepper
1 (8- to 10-pound) pork crown roast

Wild Rice Stuffing (below)
1/2 cup dry white wine
1 1/2 cups chicken stock
2 tablespoons cornstarch
2 tablespoons water

Combine the oil, thyme, allspice, salt and pepper in a small bowl and mix well. Place the pork on a rack in a roasting pan. Rub with the spice mixture. Fill the center of the pork crown roast with Wild Rice Stuffing. Place in a 450-degree oven. Bake for 15 minutes. Reduce the oven temperature to 250 degrees. Bake for 2 to 3 hours or until a meat thermometer inserted in the thickest portion registers 155 to 160 degrees.

Remove the pork to a cutting board and cover loosely with foil. Skim the pan juices. Pour the remaining pan juices into a medium saucepan. Add the wine and chicken stock. Bring to a boil and reduce heat to medium. Whisk the cornstarch into the water in a bowl. Whisk into the hot mixture. Cook until thickened, whisking constantly. Adjust the seasonings to taste. To serve, cut the pork into chops. Serve with the gravy and Wild Rice Stuffing.

Wild Rice Stuffing

YIELD: 6 TO 8 SERVINGS

1 large onion, finely chopped
1/4 cup olive oil
1 garlic clove, minced
1 pound ground pork
1/2 cup chopped fresh mint leaves, or to taste

1 cup dried sour cherries
2 tablespoons finely grated orange zest, or to taste
Salt and pepper to taste
1 cup long grain and wild rice, cooked

Sauté the onion in the oil in a nonstick skillet over low heat for 7 minutes. Add the garlic. Sauté for 3 minutes. Add the pork, mint, cherries, orange zest, salt and pepper. Cook over medium heat for 10 minutes or until brown and crumbly, stirring constantly. Cool to room temperature. Mix the rice and pork mixture in a large bowl. Use to stuff the Pork Crown Roast or spoon into a baking dish. Bake, covered with foil, at 350 degrees for 20 minutes.

Mary Ann Gray
Vera Bradley Sales Representative

Jerk Pork

The jerk seasoning has a unique Caribbean flavor
that is very good and different.

1 medium onion, coarsely chopped
1 bunch green onions, coarsely
   chopped
3 garlic cloves
2 jalapeño chiles, seeded
3 tablespoons fresh thyme, or
   1 teaspoon dried thyme
1 1/2 tablespoons brown sugar

1 1/2 teaspoons salt
1 1/2 teaspoons pepper
1 1/2 teaspoons ground allspice
3/4 teaspoon cinnamon
1/4 teaspoon ground nutmeg
2 (3-pound) rolled boneless pork loin
   roasts or tenderloins

Process the onion, green onions, garlic, chiles, thyme, brown sugar, salt, pepper, allspice, cinnamon and nutmeg in a food processor until finely chopped. Place the pork in a large sealable plastic food storage bag. Add the marinade and seal the bag. Marinate in the refrigerator for up to 2 days before grilling.

Drain the pork, discarding the marinade. Place the pork on a grill rack. Grill until a meat thermometer inserted in the thickest portion registers 185 degrees.

Dede Hall
Vera Bradley Classic Volunteer

Pork Chop Casserole

1 (16-ounce) can Chinese vegetables,
   drained
1 (10-ounce) can golden mushroom
   or cream of mushroom soup
1 1/4 cups water

1 (6-ounce) package long grain and
   wild rice mix
Pepper to taste
6 lean medium pork chops

Combine the vegetables, soup, water, rice and pepper in a large bowl and mix well. Pour into a large baking dish. Arrange the pork chops on top. Bake, covered, at 350 degrees for 1 hour and 20 minutes or until the pork is cooked through.

Nancy Adams
Vera Bradley Sales Representative

Sausage and Bean Casserole

YIELD: 8 SERVINGS

This is a consistent favorite at our Vera Bradley "carry-ins."
It also makes a great side dish.

1 pound bulk sausage	1 pound butter beans, drained
8 ounces bacon, chopped	1 pound red beans, drained
2 onions, chopped	1 cup ketchup
2 pounds pork and beans, partially drained	1 cup packed brown sugar
	Salt and pepper to taste

Brown the sausage, bacon and onions in a large skillet, stirring until the sausage is crumbly; partially drain. Add the pork and beans, butter beans, red beans, ketchup, brown sugar, salt and pepper and mix well. Pour into a large baking dish. Bake at 350 degrees for 1 hour.

Diane Brown
Vera Bradley Shipping Team

Grilled Chicken

YIELD: 4 TO 6 SERVINGS

The marinade makes this grilled chicken very tender and quite delicious.

4 to 6 chicken breasts	1 garlic clove, crushed
1/2 cup vegetable oil	1 tablespoon dry mustard
1/3 cup soy sauce	1/2 tablespoon parsley
1/4 cup white wine vinegar	1/2 teaspoon salt
2 tablespoons Worcestershire sauce	Pepper to taste
1/4 cup lemon juice	

Place the chicken in a shallow glass dish. Combine the oil, soy sauce, vinegar, Worcestershire sauce, lemon juice, garlic, dry mustard, parsley, salt and pepper in a large glass measure and mix well. Pour over the chicken. Marinate, covered, in the refrigerator for 8 to 12 hours.

Drain the chicken, reserving the marinade. Place the reserved marinade in a small saucepan. Bring to a boil. Boil for 2 to 3 minutes, stirring constantly. Place the chicken on a grill rack. Grill over medium hot coals for 5 to 6 minutes. Brush both sides with the cooked marinade. Grill for 5 minutes longer or until the juices run clear.

Patti Pine
Vera Bradley Sales Representative Coordinator

Chicken Elizabeth

YIELD: 6 SERVINGS

This is a version of Chicken Cordon Bleu that we have found
even better—the sauce makes the difference.

6 boneless chicken breasts
Salt and pepper to taste
6 ham slices
6 Swiss cheese slices

2 cups cornflakes, crushed
2 teaspoons oregano
White Wine Sauce (below)

Season the chicken with salt and pepper. Place 1 ham slice and 1 cheese
slice on each chicken breast. Roll up and tie with string. Coat with a mixture
of cornflake crumbs and oregano. Place in a shallow baking dish. Bake at
350 degrees for 45 minutes. Remove the string. Pour White Wine Sauce over
the chicken. Bake for 45 minutes longer.

White Wine Sauce

YIELD: 6 SERVINGS

2 tablespoons butter or margarine
2 tablespoons flour
2 cups chicken broth

$1/2$ cup white wine
1 cup sour cream

Melt the butter in a small saucepan over medium heat. Add the flour. Cook
until bubbly, stirring constantly. Add the broth gradually, whisking constantly.
Add the wine and sour cream. Cook until thickened, whisking constantly.

Becky Bennett
Vera Bradley Product Development Team

Chicken Piccata

A perfect mixture of chicken, mushrooms and lemons. Very delicious.

4 boneless skinless chicken breasts
Salt and pepper taste
2 tablespoons flour
2 tablespoons olive oil
1 cup sliced fresh mushrooms
1/3 cup dry white wine
1/4 cup fresh lemon juice

1 1/2 tablespoons flour
1/4 cup canned reduced-sodium
   chicken broth
1/4 cup capers, drained
1/4 cup fresh parsley, chopped
2 tablespoons butter or margarine,
   melted

Place the chicken between 2 large sheets of plastic wrap. Flatten the chicken to 1/4-inch thickness with a meat mallet or rolling pin. Sprinkle with salt and pepper. Dredge the chicken in 2 tablespoons flour in a shallow dish until coated, shaking off the excess.

Heat the oil in a large heavy skillet. Add the chicken and mushrooms. Cook the chicken for 3 minutes on each side or until the chicken is golden brown and the juices run clear. Remove the chicken to a platter and tent with foil to keep warm.

Add the wine and lemon juice to the mushrooms in the skillet. Bring to a boil. Whisk 1 1/2 tablespoons flour into the chicken broth. Add to the mushroom mixture. Cook for 2 minutes or until slightly thickened, stirring constantly. Stir in the capers, parsley and butter. Season with salt and pepper. Pour over the chicken and serve.

Stefanie Chevillet
Vera Bradley Customer Service

Roasted Whole Lemon Chickens

2 (3-pound) chickens
2 large lemons
2 teaspoons salt
1 teaspoon pepper
1 tablespoon oregano

4 garlic cloves, crushed
1/4 cup olive oil
2/3 cup fresh lemon juice
2/3 cup chicken broth
1/4 cup olive oil

Pat the chickens dry inside and outside with paper towels. Discard any excess fat. Pierce the lemons at 1/4-inch intervals. Place 1 lemon in the cavity of each chicken.

Mix the salt, pepper, oregano, garlic and 1/4 cup oil in a small bowl to form a paste. Rub over the chickens. Place the chickens breast side up side by side in a large roasting or baking pan.

Blend the lemon juice, broth and 1/4 cup oil in a bowl. Pour over the chickens. Bake at 500 degrees for 20 minutes. Turn the chickens. Roast for 20 minutes. Reduce the oven temperature to 450 degrees. Turn the chickens. Bake for 20 minutes or until the juices run clear.

Place the chickens on a cutting board. Let stand for 10 to 15 minutes. Remove the lemons from the chickens. Cut the chickens into quarters with kitchen shears. Cut the lemons into halves and squeeze over the chickens.

Mercedes Cox
Friend of Vera Bradley Designs

Baked Pineapple Chicken

YIELD: 6 SERVINGS

1 (20-ounce) can pineapple slices
1 garlic clove, crushed
2 teaspoons cornstarch
2 teaspoons Worcestershire sauce

2 teaspoons Dijon mustard
1 teaspoon crushed rosemary
6 boneless chicken breasts
1 lemon, thinly sliced

Drain the pineapple, reserving the juice. Combine the reserved juice with garlic, cornstarch, Worcestershire sauce, Dijon mustard and rosemary in a bowl and mix well. Arrange the chicken in a shallow baking dish or broiler pan. Broil until brown. Pour the sauce over the chicken. Bake at 400 degrees for 30 minutes. Arrange the lemon and pineapple slices around the chicken. Baste with the sauce from the baking pan. Bake for 5 minutes longer. Serve immediately.

Debbie Wilson
Vera Bradley Executive Administrative Assistant

Sesame Chicken Kabobs

YIELD: 6 SERVINGS

6 boneless skinless chicken breasts
1/4 cup plus 2 tablespoons
    teriyaki sauce
1/4 cup soy sauce
3 tablespoons vegetable oil
2 tablespoons dark sesame oil

2 tablespoons sesame seeds
2 medium red bell peppers, cut into
    bite-size pieces
2 medium yellow bell peppers, cut into
    bite-size pieces
2 to 3 Vidalia onions, quartered

Cut the chicken into 1-inch pieces. Arrange in a shallow baking dish. Combine the teriyaki sauce, soy sauce, vegetable oil, sesame oil and sesame seeds in a bowl and mix well. Pour over the chicken. Marinate, covered, in the refrigerator for 3 hours or longer.

Drain the chicken, reserving the marinade. Bring the reserved marinade to a boil in a small saucepan. Boil for 2 to 3 minutes, stirring constantly.

Thread the chicken alternately with the red and yellow bell peppers and onions onto skewers. Place on a grill rack. Grill over medium hot coals for 5 to 7 minutes or until the chicken juices run clear, turning and basting with the cooked marinade.

Nancy Pishney
Creative Needle Arts, Ltd.
Traverse City, Michigan

Lila's Chicken

If you've ever been to the Baekgaard's for dinner . . . you've had this!

8 ounces vermicelli
1/2 cup (1 stick) butter
1 large onion, chopped
1 1/2 cups fresh mushrooms, or
   1 medium can mushrooms
1 (10-ounce) can cream of chicken
   soup
1 (10-ounce) can cream of
   mushroom soup

2 cups chicken broth
4 boneless skinless chicken breasts,
   cut into bite-size pieces
2 cups sour cream
Seasoned pepper to taste
1 1/2 cups shredded Cheddar cheese
1/2 cup grated Parmesan cheese
5 slices rye bread, cut into cubes

Cook the pasta in boiling water to cover for 2 minutes; drain.

Melt the butter in a large skillet. Add the onion. Sauté until translucent. Combine the sautéed onion, mushrooms, soups, chicken broth and uncooked chicken in a large bowl and mix well. Add the sour cream, seasoned pepper and 1 cup of the Cheddar cheese. Stir in the slightly cooked pasta.

Spoon into a greased 8×12-inch baking dish. Sprinkle with the Parmesan cheese and the remaining 1/2 cup Cheddar cheese. Sprinkle the bread cubes over the top. Bake at 350 degrees for 1 hour or until the chicken is cooked through.

Lila Pursley
The Depot
Harbor Springs, Michigan

Grandma Beebe's Chicken Casserole

YIELD: 10 SERVINGS

This recipe is best made the day before serving and refrigerated.
Dad and the kids love to make it—the kids love to crush the cornflakes with
a rolling pin in a plastic food storage bag.

4 cups chopped cooked chicken
2 (10-ounce) cans cream of chicken
  soup
1 cup mayonnaise or reduced-fat
  mayonnaise
6 hard-cooked eggs, chopped
2¹/₂ cups cooked rice

2 cups chopped celery
2 teaspoons grated onion
2 tablespoons lemon juice
1 teaspoon salt
2 cups crushed cornflakes
¹/₄ cup butter, melted

Combine the chicken, soup, mayonnaise, eggs, rice, celery, onion, lemon
juice and salt in a large bowl and mix well. Spoon into a buttered 9×13-inch
baking dish.

Toss the cornflakes with the butter in a bowl until coated. Spread over the
chicken mixture.

Bake at 375 degrees for 30 to 40 minutes or until bubbly.

Jill Nichols
Vera Bradley Executive Vice President/COO

MAC's Chicken and Ham Casserole

"Mac" is my mother's nickname from high school. Her maiden name was
Mary Ann Clifford (now Cottrell!). All her friends, and my Dad, still
call her "Mac," and this casserole is a family favorite!

3 cups chopped cooked chicken
1 1/2 cups chopped cooked ham
8 ounces fresh mushrooms, sliced
1 (5-ounce) can sliced water
  chestnuts, drained
1/2 cup chopped onion
1/2 teaspoon salt
1/8 teaspoon pepper

2 (10-ounce) cans cream of
  chicken soup
1 cup mayonnaise
1/4 cup sherry
1 cup Swiss cheese
1/2 cup bread crumbs
3 tablespoons butter or margarine,
  melted

Combine the chicken, ham, mushrooms, water chestnuts, onion, salt and
pepper in a large bowl and mix well. Mix the soup, mayonnaise and sherry in a
bowl. Add to the chicken mixture and mix well. Stir in the cheese. Spoon into
a buttered large baking dish. Sprinkle with bread crumbs. Pour the butter over
the top. Bake at 350 degrees for 30 to 35 minutes or until bubbly.

Barb Erhardt
Vera Bradley Product Development Coordinator

Nutty Chicken Casserole

This is a Miller family favorite. It's delicious, easy and
can be made a day before serving.

3 cups chopped cooked chicken
2 cups chopped celery
1 cup cooked white rice
3/4 cup mayonnaise
1 teaspoon lemon juice
3 hard-cooked eggs, sliced
1 cup drained sliced water chestnuts

1 tablespoon minced onion
1 (10-ounce) can cream of
  mushroom soup
Freshly ground pepper to taste
1 cup slivered almonds
1 cup butter cracker crumbs
1/2 cup (1 stick) margarine, melted

Mix the chicken, celery, rice, mayonnaise, lemon juice, eggs, water chestnuts,
onion and soup in a large bowl. Spoon into a 9×13-inch baking dish. Sprinkle
with pepper. Toss the almonds and cracker crumbs in the margarine in a bowl.
Spread over the top. Bake at 350 degrees for 30 to 40 minutes or until bubbly.

Patricia R. Miller
President and Co-Founder of Vera Bradley

Swiss Chicken Casserole

Being a connoisseur of Miracle Whip, I was eager to try this recipe. When
the Swiss Chickens finally arrived, the results were delicious. This casserole
has become a favorite at carry-ins . . . must be those *special chickens!*

4 to 5 boneless skinless chicken breasts
2 cups chicken stock
2 tablespoons margarine
1 medium onion, chopped
2 cups chopped celery
2 cups croutons

1 cup shredded Swiss cheese
1 cup Miracle Whip or mayonnaise
1/2 cup milk
1 teaspoon salt
1/4 teaspoon pepper
1/4 cup walnut pieces

Poach the chicken in the chicken stock in a large skillet until the juices run
clear; drain. Remove the chicken from the skillet. Let stand until cool enough
to handle. Chop enough chicken to measure 4 cups.
   Melt the margarine in the skillet. Add the onion and celery. Sauté until
tender. Combine the chicken, sautéed vegetables, croutons, Swiss cheese,
Miracle Whip, milk, salt and pepper in a large bowl and mix well. Pour into a
large baking dish. Sprinkle with the walnuts. Bake at 350 degrees for 40 minutes.

Nieta Van Engelenhoven
Vera Bradley Production Team

Chicken and Wild Rice Casserole

YIELD: 10 SERVINGS

If you have six dinner parties a year, you'll serve this at five of them . . . it's that good! This is a continual favorite in my family and is perfect for a fall or winter dinner. The leftovers are great, and this casserole can be frozen!

1 (6-ounce) package wild rice
1 pound bulk sausage
1 (6-ounce) can mushrooms, drained
2 (10-ounce) cans cream of
  mushroom soup
1 tablespoon Worcestershire sauce

3/4 teaspoon marjoram
4 boneless skinless chicken breasts,
  poached, cut into 1-inch pieces
1 1/2 cups dry rye bread crumbs
1/4 cup (1/2 stick) butter, melted

Prepare the rice using the package directions. Brown the sausage in a skillet, stirring until crumbly; drain. Stir in the cooked rice, mushrooms, soup, Worcestershire sauce and marjoram.

Spoon 1/2 of the rice mixture into a 9×13-inch baking dish. Arrange the chicken over the rice mixture. Spoon the remaining rice mixture over the chicken. Toss the bread crumbs and butter in a bowl. Spread over the top. Bake at 375 degrees for 35 to 45 minutes or until bubbly. Do not substitute instant rice for the wild rice in this recipe.

Amy Ray
Granddaughter of Vera Bradley

Citrus-Marinated Turkey Breast

YIELD: 10 SERVINGS

It's hard to say which way is best but, grilled or roasted, this is
a sensational twist on the standard holiday bird.

1 (6- to 7-pound) turkey breast	1 jalapeño chile, seeded, minced
1 cup orange juice	2 teaspoons oregano
1/4 cup lime juice	2 teaspoons salt
1/4 cup olive oil	1 teaspoon pepper
3 tablespoons apple cider vinegar	

Remove the skin and bone from the turkey and discard. Place the turkey in a
large sealable plastic food storage bag.

Combine the orange juice, lime juice, oil, vinegar, chile, oregano, salt and
pepper in a jar with a tight-fitting lid. Cover and shake well. Reserve 1/2 cup of
the marinade. Pour the remaining marinade over the turkey and seal the bag.
Marinate in the refrigerator for 8 to 12 hours, turning occasionally.

Drain the turkey, discarding the marinade. Place on a grill rack. Grill
over hot coals for 18 minutes per side or until a meat thermometer registers
170 degrees, brushing occasionally with the reserved marinade. Let stand for
10 minutes before slicing. Garnish with fresh sage, oregano and rosemary sprigs.
You may place the turkey on a rack in a roasting pan and bake at 325 degrees
for 1 hour and 10 minutes or until the turkey tests done.

Mercedes Cox
Friend of Vera Bradley Designs

Grilled Turkey with Stuffing and Mushroom Gravy

My husband Bryan and I call this "Mercury Turkey." The first time I grilled it, I left the meat thermometer in and put the grill lid on. The thermometer exploded and we had to throw the whole thing out. That same day, we bought a new grill with a built-in temperature gauge. Turkey #2 came out *great*.

1 1/2 tablespoons rosemary
1 tablespoon pepper
2 teaspoons salt
1 1/2 teaspoons thyme
1 1/2 teaspoons tarragon

1 (20- to 21-pound) turkey
Mom's Traditional Stuffing
  (page 129)
2 tablespoons vegetable oil
Mushroom Gravy (page 129)

Mix the first 5 ingredients in a small bowl. Remove the giblets and neck from the turkey. Pat the turkey dry inside and outside with paper towels. Spoon Mom's Traditional Stuffing into the cavity. Tie the legs loosely to hold the shape of the turkey. Brush with the oil. Rub with the spice mixture.

Place the turkey on a grill rack. Grill over medium coals for 3 hours or until a meat thermometer registers 170 to 180 degrees and the juices run clear. Place on a large serving platter and tent with foil.

Serve with Mom's Traditional Stuffing and Mushroom Gravy.

Mushroom Gravy

YIELD: 25 SERVINGS

1/2 cup flour
1/2 cup dry red wine
3 tablespoons butter
12 ounces fresh mushrooms, sliced
2 teaspoons rosemary

4 cups (about) chicken broth
1/3 cup milk
1 teaspoon thyme
1 teaspoon tarragon
Salt and pepper to taste

Mix the flour and wine in a small bowl to form a smooth paste. Melt the butter in a large heavy saucepan over medium-high heat. Add the mushrooms and rosemary. Sauté for 3 minutes or until the mushrooms begin to soften.

Pour any juices from the turkey collected on the serving platter into a large glass measure. Add enough chicken broth to measure 5 cups. Add to the mushrooms. Whisk in the flour paste until smooth. Bring to a boil, stirring frequently. Cook for 10 minutes or until thickened and light brown. Stir in the milk, thyme and tarragon. Season with salt and pepper.

Kathy Reedy Ray
Vera Bradley Marketing Associate
Granddaughter of Vera Bradley

Mom's Traditional Stuffing

YIELD: 25 SERVINGS

2 tablespoons olive oil
1 cup chopped yellow onion
2 garlic cloves, minced
1 cup chopped celery
1 1/2 cups sliced mushrooms
2 tablespoons pepper

2 teaspoons salt
1 teaspoon sage
1 teaspoon celery salt
1 teaspoon thyme
4 loaves white bread, toasted, cubed
3 cups (about) chicken broth

Heat the oil in a stockpot over medium-high heat. Add the onion, garlic and celery. Sauté for 10 minutes or until tender. Add the mushrooms, pepper, salt, sage, celery salt and thyme. Cook for 5 minutes. Add the bread cubes and mix well. Add enough of the broth to moisten to the desired consistency, stirring constantly.

Use to stuff the cavity of a 20- to 21-pound turkey. Spoon any remaining dressing into a large baking dish. Scoop out the stuffing from the cavity of the cooked turkey and add to the remaining stuffing. Bake at 350 degrees for 30 minutes before serving.

Becky Bennett
Vera Bradley Product Development Team

Jalapeño Grilled Fish

YIELD: 3 SERVINGS

3 tablespoons chopped cilantro
2 tablespoons lime juice
1 tablespoon minced garlic
1 tablespoon minced ginger

1 tablespoon minced roasted
  jalapeño chiles
1 1/2 pounds firm white fish fillets

Combine the cilantro, lime juice, garlic, ginger and chiles in a small bowl and mix well. Place the fish on a lightly oiled grill rack. Grill, covered, for 5 minutes. Turn the fish. Spread with the cilantro mixture. Grill for 3 to 5 minutes or until the fish flakes easily with a fork. Serve with lime wedges.

David Goodman
Vera Bradley Creative Coordinator

Poached Salmon

YIELD: 6 SERVINGS

Poaching the salmon in the seltzer water as opposed to regular tap water gives the salmon a flavorful zip—it's very refreshing.

2 tablespoons green peppercorns
1 shallot, sliced
1 (3-pound) whole salmon, filleted

1 cup white wine
1 1/2 cups lemon seltzer (such as
  Perrier)

Press the peppercorns and shallot into the underside of the fish. Place on a poaching rack in a large skillet. Add enough wine and seltzer to come about halfway up the side of the fish.

Bring the liquid to a boil. Reduce the heat to medium-low. Poach, partly covered, for 30 minutes (about 10 minutes per pound) or until the fish flakes easily with a fork. Remove the fish immediately. Serve with a dill sauce or lemon sauce.

Barbara Bradley Baekgaard
President and Co-Founder of Vera Bradley

Baked Salmon on a Bed of Leeks

YIELD: 4 SERVINGS

How could something that tastes *so* wonderful be so healthful?

4 leeks (about 1 1/2 pounds)
Salt to taste
4 (6- to 8-ounce) salmon fillets
2 tablespoons fresh lime juice
1 tablespoon olive oil
4 teaspoons honey

1 tablespoon finely minced fresh ginger
Pepper to taste
2 tablespoons fresh lime juice
3 tablespoons olive oil
2 tablespoons snipped fresh chives
4 lime halves

Trim the leeks, leaving 3 inches of green. Cut into julienne strips. Rinse under cold running water; drain. Bring a large stockpot of salted water to a boil. Add the leeks. Blanch for 2 minutes; drain.

Arrange the fish in a single layer in a glass dish. Whisk 2 tablespoons lime juice, 1 tablespoon oil, honey, ginger, salt and pepper in a small bowl. Pour over the fish. Marinate, covered, in the refrigerator for 30 minutes, turning once. Do not marinate any longer as the citrus juice will toughen the fish.

Drain the fish, discarding the marinade. Toss the leeks with 2 tablespoons lime juice and 3 tablespoons oil. Season with salt and pepper. Arrange evenly over the bottom of a 9×13-inch baking dish. Arrange the fish skin side down over the leeks. Bake at 450 degrees for 15 minutes or until the fish flakes easily. Sprinkle with the chives. Top with the lime halves.

Sue Britton
Vera Bradley Marketing Manager

Spice-Crusted Salmon with Salsa

YIELD: 4 SERVINGS

This is a nice change from the usual salmon dishes.

Sections of 4 navel oranges
1 small red onion, finely chopped
1/4 cup fresh lime juice
1/4 cup chopped cilantro
1 tablespoon minced jalapeño chiles
1 garlic clove, minced

Salt and pepper to taste
1 tablespoon coriander seeds, crushed
1 tablespoon cumin seeds, crushed
1/2 tablespoon black peppercorns
1 teaspoon kosher salt
4 salmon fillets, skinned

Combine the oranges, onion, lime juice, cilantro, chiles, garlic, salt and pepper in a bowl and toss to mix well. Chill, covered, in the refrigerator.

Mix the coriander seeds, cumin seeds, peppercorns and kosher salt in a small bowl. Rub on the fish. Place on a grill or broiler rack. Grill or broil for 4 minutes per side or until the fish flakes easily. Serve immediately with the salsa.

Lyn Killoran
Friend of Vera Bradley

Salmon Napoleon

YIELD: 2 SERVINGS

7 ounces salmon fillets
2 pounds fresh spinach, trimmed
1 garlic clove, minced

3 tablespoons butter
Pepper to taste
1 envelope hollandaise sauce mix

Place the salmon on a rack in a baking pan. Bake at 375 degrees for 15 minutes or until the salmon flakes easily. Sauté the spinach and garlic in the butter in a skillet until tender. Season with pepper to taste. Prepare the hollandaise sauce using the package directions.

Split the salmon fillets into halves lengthwise. Place the spinach mixture on half the fillet halves. Cover with the remaining halves. Spoon hollandaise sauce over the top.

Patti Reedy
Vera Bradley Sales Representative
Granddaughter of Vera Bradley

Pacific Salmon Loaf

YIELD: 6 TO 8 SERVINGS

1 (16-ounce) can Pacific salmon,
  drained, flaked
1/2 cup dry bread crumbs
1/2 cup mayonnaise
1/2 cup chopped onion
1/2 cup chopped celery
1 egg, lightly beaten

1 teaspoon salt
2 tablespoons each butter and flour
2 cups milk
Salt and pepper to taste
1 (10-ounce) package frozen
  green peas
1/3 cup minced onion

Combine the salmon, bread crumbs, mayonnaise, 1/2 cup onion, celery, egg and 1 teaspoon salt in a large bowl and mix lightly. Shape into a loaf and place in a nonstick 5×9-inch baking pan. Bake at 350 degrees for 40 minutes.

Melt the butter in a medium saucepan. Whisk in the flour. Cook until lightly browned, whisking constantly. Whisk in the milk gradually. Cook until thickened, stirring constantly. Season with salt and pepper to taste. Stir in the peas and 1/3 cup onion. Serve immediately over the salmon loaf.

Darcie Lentz
Vera Bradley Classic Volunteer

Foxy Loxburgers

YIELD: 8 SERVINGS

Why have a regular burger? These are not only healthy, but *very* delicious!

1 1/2 pounds fresh salmon, boned,
  skinned, ground
1 teaspoon fresh lemon juice
1 tablespoon minced yellow onion
1 tablespoon minced fresh dillweed, or
  1 teaspoon dried dillweed
1 tablespoon dry sherry

1/4 teaspoon Tabasco sauce
3 ounces cream cheese, softened
1 tablespoon unsalted butter, melted
2 tablespoons capers, drained
1 teaspoon lemon juice
1/8 teaspoon Tabasco sauce

Combine the fish, 1 teaspoon lemon juice, onion, dillweed, sherry and 1/4 teaspoon Tabasco sauce in a large bowl and mix well. Divide into 8 equal portions. Shape each portion into flat round patties. Place on a grill rack. Grill over medium heat for 4 minutes or until brown on the bottom. Turn the patties. Grill for 4 to 6 minutes or until the fish is opaque.

Combine the cream cheese, butter, capers, 1 teaspoon lemon juice and 1/8 teaspoon Tabasco sauce in a small bowl and mix well. Place the fish on serving plates. Top each serving with a dollop of the cream cheese mixture.

Nancy Ecclestone
Friend of Vera Bradley

Lemon Stuffed Sole Fillets

YIELD: 4 SERVINGS

1/3 cup butter
1/3 cup chopped celery
2 tablespoons chopped onion
1 cup herb-seasoned stuffing mix
1 tablespoon parsley
1 tablespoon lemon juice

1 teaspoon lemon zest
Salt and pepper to taste
1 pound sole fillets
1/3 cup butter
1/2 teaspoon dillweed

Melt 1/3 cup butter in a small saucepan over medium heat. Add the celery and onion. Sauté until tender. Stir in the stuffing mix, parsley, lemon juice, lemon zest, salt and pepper. Remove from heat.

Arrange 1/2 of the fillets in a 9×9-inch baking pan. Top each fillet with 1/4 cup stuffing mixture. Top with the remaining fillets. Drizzle with 1/3 cup butter. Sprinkle with the dillweed. Bake at 350 degrees for 20 to 30 minutes or until the fish flakes easily with a fork.

Joan Bond
Vera Bradley Classic Steering Committee

Champagne Shrimp

Murphy, Jeannine's daughter, serves this every Christmas Eve—it has become a family favorite and tradition. She usually triples the recipe.

2 pounds shrimp, peeled, deveined
4 scallions, minced
1 1/3 cups Champagne
1/2 teaspoon salt

1/2 cup heavy cream
1/2 cup (1 stick) butter
Hot cooked rice

Combine the shrimp, scallions, Champagne and salt in a skillet. Bring to a boil and reduce heat to medium. Simmer, covered, for 10 minutes. Remove the shrimp to a warm plate and tent with foil to keep warm.

Whisk the cream into the liquid in the skillet. Bring to a boil over high heat. Cook until the mixture is reduced to 2/3 cup, whisking constantly. Whisk in the butter 1 tablespoon at a time. Return the shrimp to the skillet. Sauté for 2 minutes or until heated through. Serve the shrimp over hot cooked rice, ladling the sauce over the top.

Jeannine Wallace
Shop of the Gulls
Charlevoix, Michigan

Curry-Crusted Shrimp with Cilantro and Lime

1 1/2 pounds large shrimp, peeled,
   deveined
1 teaspoon dark rum
1 teaspoon sugar
1/8 teaspoon salt

1/3 cup mild curry powder
3 tablespoons olive oil
Cilantro leaves
2 limes, cut into wedges

Pat the shrimp dry with paper towels and place in a bowl. Sprinkle with the rum. Let stand for 20 minutes. Pat dry with paper towels. Sprinkle the shrimp evenly with sugar and salt. Sprinkle with the curry powder to form a light coating. Shake off the excess.

Heat a large nonstick skillet over medium heat. Add 1 tablespoon of the oil. Heat for 30 seconds. Add enough shrimp to cover the bottom of the skillet in a single layer. Cook for 2 minutes on each side or until brown and crisp. Remove to a warm platter. Repeat the process with the remaining 2 tablespoons oil and shrimp.

To serve, arrange the shrimp on a bed of cilantro leaves. Garnish with the lime wedges. Serve with wild rice.

Melanie Mauger
Vera Bradley Customer Service

Particularly tasty for a warm evening meal, or a romantic dinner for two. The very exciting mix of flavors— sweet, citrus, and a hint of spice—make this an outstanding and unusual dish. Serve with Grapefruit Margaritas (page 50) for an extra-special touch!

Gulf Shrimp Beer Boil

YIELD: 4 SERVINGS

Phil coordinated and illustrated *The Best of Sanibel-Captiva Restaurants* cookbook for the island's Chamber of Commerce. He thinks any recipe with "beer" in the title is a great guy dish.

2 quarts beer	1 teaspoon salt
1 medium onion, *thinly sliced*	1 teaspoon crushed dried red peppers
1 thick lemon slice	1 teaspoon thyme
4 black peppercorns	1/2 teaspoon fennel seeds
3 sprigs parsley	2 pounds unpeeled fresh Gulf shrimp
1 bay leaf	

Bring the beer, onion, lemon, peppercorns, parsley, bay leaf, salt, red peppers, thyme and fennel seeds to a boil in a deep heavy stockpot. Add the shrimp. Cook for 3 to 4 minutes or until the shrimp turn pink; drain. Discard the bay leaf. Peel the shrimp and place in a bowl. Chill, covered, in the refrigerator until serving time. Serve with your favorite sauce.

Phil Johnson
Ile Crocodile
Sanibel Island, Florida

White Lasagna

YIELD: 4 TO 6 SERVINGS

This is a great alternative to the traditional lasagna.

6 uncooked lasagna noodles	1/8 teaspoon pepper
3 pounds chicken, cooked	1/2 cup milk or chicken broth
1 (10-ounce) can cream of celery soup	6 ounces mozzarella cheese, cut into strips
1/4 teaspoon oregano	10 ounces Velveeta cheese, cubed
1 teaspoon salt	1/3 cup grated Parmesan cheese

Cook the noodles using the package directions; drain. Chop the chicken, discarding the skin and bones. Combine the chicken, soup, oregano, salt and pepper in a bowl and mix well. Add the milk and mix well.

Alternate layers of the chicken mixture, lasagna noodles, chicken mixture and cheeses in an 8×12-inch baking dish coated with nonstick cooking spray, ending with the chicken mixture and reserving some of the cheeses for the top. Bake at 350 degrees for 40 minutes. Sprinkle with the reserved cheeses. Bake for 5 to 10 minutes or until the cheeses melt. Let stand for 10 minutes.

Thirza Youker
Vera Bradley Customer Service—Retired

World's Best Lasagna

YIELD: 8 SERVINGS

I have tried many lasagna recipes and this is definitely the best.

1 pound ground beef
1 pound Italian sausage
1 large onion, chopped
1 garlic clove, crushed
2 teaspoons oregano
2 teaspoons basil
1 1/2 teaspoons salt
1 teaspoon pepper
2 (16-ounce) jars garden primavera spaghetti sauce (such as Healthy Choice)

15 ounces reduced-fat ricotta cheese
16 ounces cottage cheese
2/3 cup grated Parmesan cheese
1 egg
2 (10-ounce) packages frozen chopped spinach, thawed
10 uncooked lasagna noodles
1/2 cup shredded provolone cheese
2 tablespoons grated Parmesan cheese
1 1/2 cups shredded provolone cheese

Brown the ground beef and sausage in a large skillet, stirring until crumbly. Add the onion and garlic. Sauté for 10 minutes or until tender. Season with oregano, basil, salt and pepper. Stir in the spaghetti sauce. Simmer, uncovered, for 15 minutes.

Mix the ricotta cheese, cottage cheese, 2/3 cup Parmesan cheese, egg and spinach in a medium bowl.

Ladle 1 1/2 cups of the sauce into an 8×12-inch baking pan. Cover with 5 uncooked lasagna noodles. Spread 1/2 of the cheese and spinach mixture over the noodles. Sprinkle with 1/2 cup provolone cheese and 2 tablespoons Parmesan cheese. Continue layering with 1/2 of the remaining sauce, remaining lasagna noodles, remaining cheese and spinach mixture, 1/2 cup of the remaining provolone cheese, remaining Parmesan cheese and remaining sauce.

Bake at 350 degrees for 45 minutes. Sprinkle with the remaining 1 cup provolone cheese. Bake for 15 minutes or until the cheese bubbles and is light brown. Let stand for 5 minutes before serving.

Stefanie Chevillet
Vera Bradley Customer Service

South-of-the-Border Lasagna

YIELD: 10 SERVINGS

This is a great alternative to tacos—especially if you are looking for something a little more nutritious and substantial for your family dinner.

1 pound lean ground beef
1 onion, chopped
1 garlic clove, minced
2 tablespoons chili powder
3 cups tomato sauce
1/2 cup water
1 teaspoon sugar
1 tablespoon salt

1 (6-ounce) can sliced black olives, drained
2 cups small curd cottage cheese
1 egg, lightly beaten
8 ounces pepper Jack cheese, shredded
10 corn tortillas
2 cups shredded Cheddar cheese

Brown the ground beef in a skillet over medium-high heat, stirring until crumbly; drain. Add the onion. Sauté for 5 minutes or until tender. Add the garlic. Sauté for 1 minute. Sprinkle with the chili powder. Add the tomato sauce, water, sugar, salt and olives. Simmer, uncovered, for 15 minutes.

Combine the cottage cheese and egg in a bowl and mix well.

Spread 1/3 of the sauce in a 9×13-inch baking dish sprayed with nonstick cooking spray. Layer the pepper-Jack cheese, cottage cheese mixture, corn tortillas and remaining sauce 1/2 at a time in the prepared dish. Cover with the Cheddar cheese.

Bake at 350 degrees for 30 minutes or until bubbly. Let stand for 15 minutes. Cut into squares. Serve with chopped tomatoes, shredded lettuce, salsa and sour cream.

Amy Ray
Granddaughter of Vera Bradley

Jambalaya Pasta

YIELD: 4 SERVINGS

Although this recipe has a lot of ingredients in it, it is definitely worth your time and energy. Your family will appreciate it.

1 cup finely chopped onion
1 cup finely chopped green bell pepper
1 cup finely chopped celery
2 garlic cloves, minced
2 tablespoons olive oil
1 (14-ounce) can tomatoes, chopped
1 cup chicken broth
1 (6-ounce) can tomato paste
1 teaspoon crushed oregano
1/2 teaspoon crushed basil
1/2 teaspoon crushed thyme

1/4 teaspoon cayenne pepper
1/4 teaspoon black pepper
8 ounces andouille, cooked
12 large shrimp, cooked, peeled, deveined
1 cup chopped cooked ham
8 ounces uncooked bow tie pasta
8 drops of Tabasco sauce, or to taste
1/4 cup snipped parsley
1/2 cup grated Parmesan cheese

Cook the onion, bell pepper, celery and garlic in the oil in a large saucepan for 5 to 7 minutes or until tender; drain. Add the tomatoes, broth and tomato paste. Stir in the oregano, basil, thyme, cayenne pepper and black pepper. Simmer, covered, for 20 minutes. Add the sausage, shrimp and ham. Cook until heated through.

Cook the pasta using the package directions; drain. Combine the pasta, shrimp sauce, Tabasco sauce and parsley in a large serving bowl and toss gently to mix. Sprinkle with the Parmesan cheese before serving.

Patti Pine
Vera Bradley Sales Representative Coordinator

Spaghetti Pie

This recipe freezes well. Double the recipe and make one
for now and freeze one for later.

6 ounces spaghetti
2 eggs, lightly beaten
1/4 cup grated Parmesan cheese
2 tablespoons butter
1 cup sliced mushrooms
1/3 cup chopped onion

1 cup sour cream
1 pound bulk sausage
1 (6-ounce) can tomato paste
1 cup water
4 ounces mozzarella cheese, shredded

Cook the spaghetti using the package directions; drain. Combine the hot pasta,
eggs and Parmesan cheese in a large bowl and toss to coat well. Line a greased
10-inch pie plate with the spaghetti mixture, pressing up and around side.

Melt the butter in a large skillet. Add the mushrooms and onion. Sauté
until tender. Remove from heat. Stir in the sour cream. Spoon into the
prepared pie plate.

Wipe the skillet with a damp paper towel. Add the sausage. Brown the
sausage, stirring until crumbly; drain. Add the tomato paste and water. Simmer
for 10 minutes. Spoon over the sour cream mixture.

Bake at 350 degrees for 25 minutes. Place the mozzarella cheese over the
top. Bake until the mozzarella cheese melts and browns on top.

Palma Ashley
Vera Bradley New Accounts Coordinator

Spaghetti Sauce

1 pound ground beef
1 medium onion, chopped
1/2 cup chopped green bell pepper
1 (8-ounce) jar tomato sauce
1 (6-ounce) can tomato paste
2 tablespoons sugar

1/2 teaspoon garlic powder
1/2 teaspoon oregano
1 bay leaf
1/2 teaspoon basil
1/2 teaspoon pepper

Brown the ground beef with the onion and bell pepper in a skillet, stirring
until the ground beef is crumbly; drain. Add the tomato sauce, tomato paste,
sugar, garlic powder, oregano, bay leaf, basil and pepper. Simmer for 20 minutes.
Remove the bay leaf. Serve over spaghetti or your favorite hot cooked pasta.

Debbie Ferguson
Roanoke Country Club
Roanoke, Virginia

Stroganoff Casserole

1 pound lean ground beef
1 small onion, chopped
Juice of $1/2$ fresh lemon
1 large garlic clove
1 cup fresh mushrooms
1 (10-ounce) can cream of
  mushroom soup

$1/2$ soup can milk
2 cups sour cream
8 ounces thick egg noodles, cooked
$1/2$ cup (1 stick) butter or margarine,
  melted

Brown the ground beef and onion in a large skillet over medium-high heat, stirring until the ground beef is crumbly; drain. Sprinkle with the lemon juice. Add the garlic and mushrooms.

Whisk the soup and milk in a bowl. Stir into the ground beef mixture and reduce heat. Simmer, covered, for 20 minutes. Remove from heat. Stir in the sour cream.

Toss the noodles with the melted butter. Layer the noodles and ground beef mixture $1/3$ at a time in a greased 9×13-inch baking dish. Bake at 325 degrees for 45 minutes.

Helen Bigg
Vera Bradley Sales Representative

Pasta with Sausage and Chicken

This is an excellent pasta dish. My family loves it, especially for leftovers.

12 ounces farfalle
3 tablespoons olive oil
2 boneless skinless chicken breasts,
    cut into 1-inch pieces
1/2 cup dry white wine
1 pound hot Italian sausage, casings
    removed
2 cups chopped onions
1 red bell pepper, julienned

1 (14-ounce) can tomatoes
1 1/4 cups chicken stock
2 tablespoons tomato paste
1 tablespoon chopped fresh garlic
1 tablespoon rosemary
Salt and pepper to taste
1 1/2 cups grated Parmesan cheese
1/2 cup fresh parsley, finely chopped

Cook the pasta al dente using the package directions; drain and cool.

Heat the oil in a large stockpot over medium-high heat. Add the chicken. Sauté for 5 minutes or until cooked through. Remove the chicken to a bowl using a slotted spoon. Add the wine to the stockpot. Boil until reduced to 2 tablespoons. Pour over the chicken. Add the sausage, onions and bell pepper to the stockpot. Cook until the sausage is brown, stirring until crumbly. Stir in the undrained tomatoes, chicken stock, tomato paste, garlic and rosemary. Simmer for 10 minutes or until reduced to a sauce consistency. Stir in the undrained chicken. Cook until heated through. Season with salt and pepper.

Rinse the pasta under warm water; drain. Add to the sauce and toss to mix well. Stir in 1 cup of the Parmesan cheese and parsley. Cook for 5 to 7 minutes or until heated through. Spoon into a large serving bowl. Serve with the remaining 1/2 cup Parmesan cheese.

Stefanie Chevillet
Vera Bradley Customer Service

Creamy Chicken and Tomato Casserole

This is an updated recipe for chicken noodle casserole
that is definitely a family favorite.

3/4 cup sun-dried tomatoes
8 ounces bow tie pasta
1 tablespoon olive oil
2 green onions, sliced
1 garlic clove, minced
12 ounces boneless skinless chicken
   breasts, cut into bite-size pieces
1/4 cup dry white wine

1/4 cup chopped fresh basil
1 tablespoon chopped fresh Italian
   flat-leaf parsley
1 (10-ounce) jar light Alfredo sauce
1/3 cup milk
1/4 cup grated Parmesan cheese
1/4 teaspoon pepper
1/4 cup grated Parmesan cheese

Soak the sun-dried tomatoes in water to cover in a bowl; drain well and pat dry. Cut the tomatoes into slices; set aside. Cook the pasta using the package directions; drain well.

Heat the oil in a large skillet over medium-high heat. Add the green onions and garlic and sauté briefly. Add the chicken. Sauté for 3 to 4 minutes or until the chicken is cooked through; drain well. Add the wine, basil and parsley and sauté for 1 minute.

Combine the pasta, sun-dried tomatoes, chicken mixture, Alfredo sauce, milk, 1/4 cup Parmesan cheese and pepper in a large bowl and mix well. Spoon into a 2-quart baking dish. Sprinkle with 1/4 cup Parmesan cheese.

Bake, covered, at 350 degrees for 15 minutes. Bake, uncovered, for 10 minutes longer or until heated through and light brown. Garnish with additional fresh basil.

Leslie K. Byrne
Daughter-in-law of Barbara Bradley Baekgaard

Carolina Oregano Shrimp

YIELD: 8 SERVINGS

When we travel to Hilton Head, my boyfriend and I always plan to spend some time on his dad's shrimp boat. A long day in the hot South Carolina sun naturally leads to a hearty appetite. We're continually in search of new and easy shrimp recipes to complement the day's catch. Fancy and fast, this recipe is wonderful for an "unexpected" dinner party or anytime you'd like to enjoy a light, simple shrimp dish. We recommend it with a cold beer, or light chardonnay—and a boat doesn't hurt either!

1¹/2 pounds fresh large shrimp, peeled, deveined

2 tablespoons fresh lemon juice

2 garlic cloves, minced

¹/2 cup bread crumbs

2 tablespoons freshly grated Parmesan cheese

2 tablespoons chopped fresh parsley

2 teaspoons minced fresh oregano

¹/2 cup (1 stick) unsalted butter, melted

1 pound angel hair pasta, cooked al dente

Place the shrimp in a 9×13-inch baking dish. Sprinkle with the lemon juice. Combine the garlic, bread crumbs, Parmesan cheese, parsley and oregano in a small bowl and mix well. Sprinkle over the shrimp. Drizzle the butter over the top.

Bake at 325 degrees for 10 to 15 minutes or until hot and bubbly. Serve over the angel hair pasta.

Patti Reedy
Vera Bradley Sales Representative
Granddaughter of Vera Bradley

Shrimp in Angel Hair Pasta

This is a great dish for a brunch. It can be made ahead
of time and refrigerated.

1 tablespoon butter
2 eggs
1 cup half-and-half
1 cup plain yogurt
1/2 cup shredded Swiss cheese
1/3 cup crumbled feta cheese
1/3 cup chopped parsley
1 teaspoon basil

1 teaspoon oregano
9 ounces uncooked fresh
    angel hair pasta
1 (16-ounce) jar mild thick and
    chunky salsa
1 pound medium shrimp, peeled,
    deveined
1/2 cup shredded Monterey Jack cheese

Grease an 8×12-inch baking dish with 1 tablespoon butter. Combine the eggs,
half-and-half, yogurt, Swiss cheese, feta cheese, parsley, basil and oregano in a
medium bowl and mix well.

Arrange 1/2 of the pasta in the prepared baking dish. Cover with the salsa.
Layer 1/2 of the shrimp, remaining pasta, egg mixture and remaining shrimp
over the pasta. Sprinkle with the Monterey Jack cheese. Bake at 350 degrees for
30 minutes. Let stand for 10 minutes before serving.

Jean Quinn and Pat Mallery
Country Loft
Saginaw, Michigan

Roasted Bell Pepper Pasta

YIELD: 8 SERVINGS

The fennel seeds and roasted peppers give this pasta dish a meaty flavor.

1 tablespoon olive oil
2 cups chopped onions
1/2 teaspoon fennel seeds, crushed
2 garlic cloves, minced
2 (14-ounce) cans tomatoes, chopped
1 pound green bell peppers, roasted
1 pound red bell peppers, roasted

1 pound yellow bell peppers, roasted
1/2 teaspoon salt
1/4 teaspoon pepper
6 1/2 cups tubular or bow-tie pasta,
  cooked, drained
1/2 cup fresh basil, thinly sliced
1/2 cup grated Parmesan cheese

Heat the oil in a large nonstick skillet over medium heat. Add the onions, fennel seeds and garlic. Cook, covered, for 10 minutes, stirring occasionally. Add the tomatoes. Bring to a boil and reduce heat. Simmer, uncovered, for 30 minutes, stirring occasionally.

Cut the roasted bell peppers into julienne strips. Add to the tomato mixture. Season with salt and pepper. Cook for 3 minutes or until heated through.

Combine the cooked pasta, roasted pepper mixture and basil in a large serving bowl and toss to mix well. Sprinkle with the Parmesan cheese. Serve immediately.

Kathy Reedy Ray
Vera Bradley Marketing Associate
Granddaughter of Vera Bradley

Pasta with Fresh Tomato Sauce

YIELD: 8 SERVINGS

Eddie studied at James Beard's School in New York City, at The Four Seasons, and with Simone Beck. She has served this recipe for poolside picnics and boating parties. The secret here is fresh "everything."

2 tablespoons minced garlic
1 medium onion, minced
1 tablespoon olive oil
3 pounds very ripe tomatoes, peeled, seeded, coarsely chopped
1/4 cup olive oil
1/4 cup red wine vinegar

3/4 cup fresh basil, chopped
Salt and freshly ground pepper to taste
1 pound linguini or thin spaghetti
1 tablespoon olive oil
Freshly grated Romano or Parmesan cheese to taste

Sauté the garlic and onion in 1 tablespoon oil in a small skillet over medium heat until tender; do not brown.

Place the undrained chopped tomatoes in a large glass bowl. Stir in 1/4 cup oil, vinegar and basil. Add the sautéed garlic and onion and mix well. Season with salt and pepper. Let stand, covered, at room temperature for 6 hours or chill for 8 to 12 hours in the refrigerator, bringing to room temperature before serving.

Add the pasta and 1 tablespoon oil to boiling water in a large saucepan. Cook until al dente; drain. Place the pasta in a large nonmetallic serving bowl. Add the room-temperature sauce and toss to mix well. Sprinkle with cheese.

Eddie Johnson
Ile Crocodile
Sanibel Island, Florida

Tortilla Black Bean Casserole

YIELD: 10 SERVINGS

This is a hearty vegetarian dish, but if your group prefers, you may
add 2 cups chopped cooked chicken to the bean mixture.

2 cups chopped onion
1 1/2 cups chopped green bell pepper
1 or 2 jalapeño chiles, seeded, chopped
1 (14-ounce) can chopped tomatoes
3/4 cup picante sauce
2 garlic cloves, minced

2 teaspoons cumin
2 (15-ounce) cans black beans,
  drained, rinsed
12 corn tortillas
2 cups shredded pepper-Jack cheese

Combine the onion, bell pepper, chiles, tomatoes, picante sauce, garlic
and cumin in a large skillet. Bring to a boil and reduce heat. Simmer for
10 minutes. Stir in the black beans.

Spread 1/3 of the bean mixture in a nonstick 9×13-inch glass baking dish.
Cover with 6 tortillas, overlapping as necessary. Sprinkle with 1/2 of the cheese.
Continue layering with 1/2 of the remaining bean mixture, remaining tortillas
and remaining bean mixture. Bake, covered, at 350 degrees for 30 to 35
minutes or until bubbly. Uncover and sprinkle with the remaining cheese. Let
stand for 10 minutes before serving. Serve with chopped tomatoes, shredded
lettuce and black olives.

Marta Johnson
Friend of Vera Bradley Designs

California Patty Melts

The goat cheese really sets this recipe above all other patty melts.
It is definitely worth trying.

3 tablespoons unsalted butter
2 cups thinly sliced yellow onions
1 pound ground beef
2 teaspoons Worcestershire sauce

Salt and freshly ground pepper to taste
4 ounces goat cheese
8 slices rye bread
Dijon mustard to taste

Melt the butter in a medium skillet over medium heat. Add the onions. Sauté until tender. Reduce heat to low. Cook, covered, for 15 minutes. Uncover and continue cooking for 45 minutes or until soft and golden brown. Remove from heat and keep warm.

Combine the ground beef, Worcestershire sauce, salt and pepper in a bowl and mix well. Divide into 8 equal portions. Shape each portion into thin patties. Cut the cheese into 4 pieces a little smaller than the patties. Place 1 piece of cheese on top of each of the 4 patties. Top with the remaining patties, sealing the edge to enclose the cheese.

Place on a grill rack. Grill for 4 minutes. Turn the patties. Cook for 4 minutes or until the patties are cooked through. Toast the bread slices on the outer portion of the grill rack.

To serve, layer 4 of the bread slices with the patties, onions and Dijon mustard. Top with the remaining bread slices. Serve with chips or French fries.

Amy Grinsfelder
Vera Bradley Marketing Design Coordinator

Spinach Feta Burgers

2 (10-ounce) packages frozen chopped
  spinach, thawed, drained
2 (4-ounce) packages crumbled feta
  cheese
3/4 cup Italian bread crumbs
1 medium onion, chopped
4 garlic cloves, minced
1 egg, lightly beaten
1/2 teaspoon salt

1 teaspoon black pepper
1/4 teaspoon red pepper
1/4 cup Italian bread crumbs
1 tablespoon vegetable oil
6 whole wheat buns, toasted
Ranch salad dressing to taste
6 red onion slices
6 tomato slices

Press the spinach between 2 layers of paper towels to remove the excess
moisture. Combine the spinach, cheese, 3/4 cup bread crumbs, onion, garlic,
egg, salt, black pepper and red pepper in a bowl and mix well. Divide into
6 equal portions. Shape each portion into a patty. Coat with 1/4 cup bread
crumbs. Chill, covered, for 30 minutes.

   Cook the patties in the oil in a large nonstick skillet over medium heat for
5 minutes on each side or until cooked through; drain on paper towels. Serve
on toasted buns with ranch salad dressing, red onion slices and tomato slices.
You may grill the burgers on a grill rack over medium-high heat for 3 to
5 minutes per side or until cooked through.

Debra Bleeke
Vera Bradley Customer Service

Italian Veggie Burgers

YIELD: 4 SERVINGS

This recipe comes from one of Fort Wayne's premier dining spots, Catablu Gourmet American Grille, a beautiful atmosphere to enjoy wonderful food and drink. We are also very thankful to Mike and Maureen for their involvement with the *Vera Bradley Classic* each year!

1 tablespoon olive oil
2 cups finely chopped portobello
  mushroom caps
1 cup finely chopped red bell pepper
1/2 cup finely chopped red onion
1/2 cup finely chopped asparagus
3 tablespoons chopped garlic
1 tablespoon ground fennel
1/2 teaspoon crushed red pepper
1/2 cup drained canned garbanzo
  beans
1 tablespoon olive oil

1 cup old-fashioned oats
1/2 cup finely chopped sun-dried
  tomatoes
1/2 cup finely chopped or grated
  provolone cheese
3 tablespoons chopped fresh basil
1 tablespoon olive oil
1 teaspoon salt
1/8 teaspoon black pepper
1 tablespoon olive oil
4 whole grain buns, toasted
Garlic Basil Mayonnaise (below)

Heat a large skillet over medium high heat. Add 1 tablespoon oil. Add the mushrooms, bell pepper, onion, asparagus, garlic, fennel and red pepper. Sauté for 3 to 5 minutes or until tender. Remove from heat. Cool to room temperature.

Purée the garbanzo beans with 1 tablespoon oil in a blender or food processor until smooth. Add to the cooled vegetable mixture with the oats, sun-dried tomatoes, cheese, basil, 1 tablespoon oil, salt and black pepper and mix well. Let stand for 30 minutes.

Shape into 4 patties. Fry in 1 tablespoon oil in a skillet over medium heat for 5 to 7 minutes or until heated through. Serve on the toasted buns with a dollop of Garlic Basil Mayonnaise. You may also serve with a small green salad.

Garlic Basil Mayonnaise

YIELD: 4 SERVINGS

1/2 cup mayonnaise
1/2 teaspoon minced garlic

2 tablespoons finely chopped
  fresh basil

Combine the mayonnaise, garlic and basil in a small bowl and mix well.

Mike and Maureen Catalogna
Catablu Gourmet American Grill
Fort Wayne, Indiana

Hearty Mediterranean Torte

YIELD: 8 SERVINGS

A great sandwich to serve to the guys during
halftime of the football game.

1 (32-ounce) package frozen bread
   dough, thawed
2 (10-ounce) packages frozen chopped
   spinach, thawed
1 (14-ounce) can artichoke heart
   quarters
1 (12-ounce) jar red bell pepper strips
1 (6-ounce) can pitted black olives

1 pound fresh mushrooms, sliced
8 ounces salami, thinly sliced
8 ounces provolone cheese,
   thinly sliced
8 ounces cooked ham, thinly sliced
1 egg
1 tablespoon water

Cut 1 loaf bread dough into halves crosswise. Roll one of the halves into a
10-inch circle on a lightly floured surface. Cover and set aside. Press the
remaining dough together. Roll into a 12-inch circle on a lightly floured
surface. Fit into a 9-inch springform pan, allowing the edge to overhang.

Drain the spinach, artichokes, bell peppers and olives. Press the spinach
and bell peppers between paper towels to remove the excess moisture.

Sauté the mushrooms in a nonstick skillet for 8 minutes or until soft.

Layer 1/2 of the salami, sautéed mushrooms and olives in the prepared pan.
Top with 1/2 of the cheese slices. Continue layering with 1/2 of the ham,
spinach, bell peppers, remaining salami, remaining ham and artichokes. Top
with the remaining cheese slices. Brush the overhanging dough with a mixture
of egg and water. Top the layers with the remaining dough circle. Fold the
edge over the circle, crimping as necessary and pressing to seal. Brush with the
remaining egg mixture.

Place on the bottom oven rack. Bake at 350 degrees for 30 to 35 minutes.
Remove from oven and cover with foil to prevent overbrowning if necessary.
Bake for 15 to 20 minutes longer. Cool in the pan on a wire rack. Remove the
side of the pan and cut into wedges.

Debbie Wilson
Vera Bradley Executive Administrative Assistant

Barbecued Pork Sandwiches

1 (5-pound) bone-in rump pork roast
Salt and pepper to taste
1 cup ketchup
1 cup water
1 teaspoon liquid smoke
1/4 cup cider vinegar

2 tablespoons brown sugar
1 tablespoon dry mustard
1 tablespoon Worcestershire sauce
1 garlic clove, minced
4 to 6 Kaiser rolls, toasted

Sprinkle the pork with salt and pepper. Place in a baking pan. Bake at 350 degrees for 3 hours or until the pork pulls from the bone and is cooked through. Cool until the pork is cool enough to handle. Cut the pork into bite-size pieces, discarding the skin and bone.

Combine the ketchup, water, liquid smoke, vinegar, brown sugar, dry mustard, Worcestershire sauce and garlic in a large stockpot. Bring to a low boil. Reduce heat to low. Add the pork. Cook, covered, over low heat for 2 to 3 hours or until the pork falls apart, stirring occasionally. Serve over toasted Kaiser rolls. You may add a bottle of your favorite barbecue sauce before serving for a stronger flavor.

Joyce Neubauer
Vera Bradley Classic Steering Committee

Herbed Vegetable Sandwiches with Anchovies

YIELD: 4 SERVINGS

2 large plum tomatoes, cut into
    halves, seeded
1 red onion, cut into halves vertically,
    cut into 1/2-inch-thick slices
1 red bell pepper, cored, quartered
1 zucchini, trimmed, cut lengthwise
    into 1/4-inch-thick slices
1 medium eggplant, cut into
    1/4-inch-thick half rounds

4 garlic cloves
1 1/2 tablespoons olive oil
1/4 cup chopped parsley
1 teaspoon rosemary
Salt and pepper
4 long Italian rolls
1 (2-ounce) can anchovy fillets,
    drained
2 cups watercress leaves, torn

Combine the tomatoes, onion, bell pepper, zucchini, eggplant, garlic and oil in a large roasting pan. Bake at 400 degrees for 30 minutes, stirring frequently. Stir in the parsley and rosemary. Bake for 15 minutes or until the vegetables are tender. Remove the garlic and cut into thin slices. Return to the pan. Season with salt and pepper.

Cut the rolls into halves horizontally. Place on a baking sheet. Broil until toasted. Arrange the vegetables on 1/2 of the rolls. Arrange 3 anchovies and watercress over each. Top with the remaining rolls. Cut into halves and serve.

Denise Mitchell
Vera Bradley Administrative Assistant

ON A SWEET NOTE
DESSERTS

Easy Baklava

A great alternative for those who have tried to make baklava the traditional way, this is much easier and the taste is very comparable.

3/4 cup sugar
1/2 cup water
1/2 teaspoon lemon juice
1 (16-ounce) package frozen phyllo
1 cup (2 sticks) butter

1/4 teaspoon cinnamon
1/2 cup sugar
1 cup finely chopped pecans or
    walnuts

Combine 3/4 cup sugar, water and lemon juice in a saucepan. Bring to a boil. Boil for 15 seconds. Remove from heat. Let stand until cool.

Thaw the phyllo using the package directions. Melt the butter in a small saucepan or in a microwave-safe dish in the microwave.

Unfold the phyllo. Cut into halves. Place 1 portion on a greased baking sheet. Sprinkle with the cinnamon, 1/2 cup sugar and pecans. Top with the remaining phyllo. Cut into diamond patterns with a sharp knife. Spoon the melted butter over the top. Bake at 300 degrees for 1 to 1 1/2 hours or until golden brown. Remove from oven. Pour the cooled syrup over the pastry. Let stand for 30 minutes before serving.

Cher Bond
Vera Bradley Credit Manager

Banana Split Dessert

YIELD: 15 SERVINGS

Kids love this dessert. It really does taste like a banana
split—it's just not as messy.

2 cups graham cracker crumbs
5 tablespoons butter or margarine,
    melted
8 ounces cream cheese, softened
2 cups confectioners' sugar
1 teaspoon vanilla extract
2 (16-ounce) packages fresh
    strawberries

1 (16-ounce) can crushed pineapple,
    drained
2 or 3 bananas, sliced
12 ounces whipped topping
Chopped pecans

Mix the graham cracker crumbs and butter in a bowl. Press into a 9×13-inch
dish. Chill for 1 hour.

Beat the cream cheese and confectioners' sugar in a mixing bowl until
smooth. Beat in the vanilla. Spread over the crust.

Arrange the strawberries and pineapple over the cream cheese layer.
Top with the bananas. Spread the whipped topping over the layers. Sprinkle
with pecans. Chill, covered, for 6 hours or longer before serving. You may
substitute frozen strawberries that have been thawed and drained for the
fresh strawberries.

Phyllis Loy
Vera Bradley Customer Service

Mixed Berry Crisp

This berry crisp is great served warm with a big dollop of vanilla ice cream.

3 nectarines, chopped
1 cup blueberries
1 cup sliced strawberries
1 cup raspberries
1/4 cup sugar
1 cup flour
1 tablespoon fresh lemon juice

3/4 cup old-fashioned oats
2/3 cup packed brown sugar
1 teaspoon cinnamon
1/2 teaspoon ginger
1/4 teaspoon nutmeg
1/4 teaspoon salt
7 tablespoons butter, cut into pieces

Combine the nectarines, blueberries, strawberries, raspberries, sugar, 1/4 cup of the flour and lemon juice in a large bowl and toss to mix well. Spoon into a 9-inch glass pie plate.

Mix the remaining 3/4 cup flour, oats, brown sugar, cinnamon, ginger, nutmeg and salt in a bowl. Cut in the butter until crumbly. Sprinkle over the berry mixture.

Bake at 375 degrees for 1 hour or until bubbly and the top is golden brown. Let stand for 15 minutes before serving. Serve warm or at room temperature.

Katie Burns
Friend of Vera Bradley Designs

Berry-Filled Meringue Hearts

YIELD: 2 SERVINGS

A very festive dessert for Valentine's Day.

12 hazelnuts, toasted
2 tablespoons sugar
1 egg white
1/4 teaspoon cream of tartar
1/8 teaspoon salt
2 tablespoons sugar

1 (10-ounce) package frozen
   sweetened raspberries, thawed
2 tablespoons dry red wine
1 cup strawberries, sliced
1/2 cup whipping cream, whipped

Process the hazelnuts with 2 tablespoons sugar in a food processor until finely ground. Beat the egg white, cream of tartar and salt in a mixing bowl until soft peaks form. Add 2 tablespoons sugar gradually, beating constantly until stiff peaks form. Fold in the hazelnut mixture.

Spoon 1/2 of the meringue using a rubber spatula onto a baking sheet lined with parchment paper. Shape into a heart. Repeat with the remaining meringue. Place in a preheated 300-degree oven. Reduce the oven temperature immediately to 250 degrees. Bake for 1 hour or until light brown and dry. Turn off the oven. Let stand in the closed oven for 3 hours or until completely cool. Store at room temperature in an airtight container.

Combine the undrained raspberries and wine in a bowl and toss to coat. Let stand at room temperature for 3 hours.

To serve, score a small triangle in the top center of each meringue heart; press down to form an indentation. Place each in the center of a dessert plate. Spoon the raspberry mixture into the indentations. Top with the sliced strawberries and a dollop of the whipped cream.

Denise Mitchell
Vera Bradley Administrative Assistant

Candy Bar Cheesecake

YIELD: 12 SERVINGS

If you like Mounds candy bars, you will love this cheesecake.

5 to 6 ounces chocolate wafer cookies
1 cup shredded sweetened coconut
2 tablespoons sugar
1/4 cup (1/2 stick) butter, melted
16 ounces cream cheese, softened
3/4 cup canned cream of coconut
1/2 cup shredded sweetened coconut

3 eggs
1/2 teaspoon vanilla extract
8 ounces dark sweet chocolate
2 tablespoons butter
2 tablespoons canned cream of
   coconut

Process the cookies, 1 cup coconut and sugar in a food processor until crumbly. Add 1/4 cup butter and process until combined. Pat into a 9-inch springform pan. Bake at 350 degrees for 10 minutes or until light brown. Cool on a wire rack.

Reduce the oven temperature to 300 degrees. Beat the cream cheese, 3/4 cup cream of coconut and 1/2 cup coconut in a large mixing bowl until creamy. Add the eggs 1 at a time, mixing well after each addition. Add the vanilla and stir to mix well. Pour into the cooled crust.

Fill an 8-inch pie plate with water. Place on the bottom oven rack. Place the cheesecake on the center oven rack. Bake for 1 hour or until lightly set. Let stand at room temperature for 15 minutes. Chill, covered, for 1 hour or longer.

Combine the chocolate, 2 tablespoons butter and 2 tablespoons cream of coconut in a small saucepan. Heat until melted, stirring constantly. Spread gently over the top of the cheesecake. Chill, covered, for 3 to 12 hours.

Let the cheesecake stand for 10 to 15 minutes at room temperature before serving. Uncover and remove the side of the pan. Cut into slices with a warm knife and serve.

Cher Bond
Vera Bradley Credit Manager

Lemon Swirl Cheesecake

YIELD: 12 SERVINGS

This is an elegant dessert for true lemon lovers.

6 whole graham crackers
  (about 3 ounces)
1 cup walnuts, toasted
3 tablespoons butter, melted
2 teaspoons lemon zest
16 ounces cream cheese, softened
1/2 cup sugar
1/2 cup thawed frozen lemonade
  concentrate
2 teaspoons lemon zest

3/4 cup sour cream
2 eggs
1 cup sour cream, at room
  temperature
1 (11-ounce) jar lemon curd
2/3 cup chilled whipping cream
2 (1/4-inch) lemon slices, cut into
  4 wedges each
8 small sprigs of mint

Process the graham crackers in a food processor until finely ground. Add the walnuts. Process until coarsely chopped. Add the butter and 2 teaspoons lemon zest. Process just until moistened. Press over the bottom of a 9-inch springform pan. Bake at 350 degrees for 10 minutes or until set. Cool on a wire rack.

Beat the cream cheese, sugar, lemonade concentrate and 2 teaspoons lemon zest in a large mixing bowl until smooth. Beat in 3/4 cup sour cream. Add the eggs 1 at a time, beating just until combined after each addition. Pour into the crust. Bake for 50 minutes or until the center moves slightly when the pan is shaken. Cool for 5 minutes on a wire rack.

Whisk 1 cup sour cream in a small bowl until smooth. Whisk the lemon curd in a small bowl until smooth. Run a sharp knife around the side of the cheesecake. Alternate small dollops of sour cream and lemon curd side by side in concentric circles atop the warm cheesecake, covering the top completely and starting at the outside edge. Shake the pan gently to smooth out the toppings. Swirl the toppings gently with the tip of a knife to marbleize. Chill, covered, for 8 to 12 hours.

Beat the whipping cream in a medium bowl until soft peaks form. Spoon into a pastry bag fitted with a medium star tip. Run a sharp knife around the side of the cheesecake to loosen. Release the side of the pan. Place the cheesecake on a cake platter. Pipe the whipped cream in a decorative scalloped border around the top edge. Garnish with lemon wedges and mint sprigs.

Leslie K. Byrne
Daughter-in-law of Barbara Bradley Baekgaard

Rosebud's Cheesecake Supreme

YIELD: 16 SERVINGS

This recipe is from the old Penn-Atlantic Hotel in Atlantic City.

14 zwieback cookies, crumbled
1/2 cup sugar
1/8 teaspoon cinnamon
1/2 cup (1 stick) butter, melted
48 ounces cream cheese, softened
2 1/4 cups sugar

1/4 cup plus 2 tablespoons flour
6 eggs
Juice of 1 lemon
1 teaspoon vanilla extract
1 1/2 cups light cream

Process the cookies, 1/2 cup sugar, cinnamon and butter in a food processor until combined. Reserve 2 tablespoons of the crumb mixture. Press the remaining crumb mixture over the bottom and up the side of a tube pan.

Beat the cream cheese in a mixing bowl until smooth. Add 2 1/4 cups sugar, flour, eggs, lemon juice, vanilla and cream in the order listed, beating constantly. Pour into the prepared pan. Sprinkle with the reserved crumb mixture. Bake at 325 degrees for 1 hour. Turn off oven. Cool in the closed oven for 1 hour.

Rosie Welsh
Rosebud's
Aspinwall, Pennsylvania

Cheesecakes often fall prey to a particular baking mishap—cracking. To prevent this, try baking the cheesecake in the following manner: After filling the cheesecake pan, wrap it tightly in foil and place it in a large roasting pan. Pour boiling water in the roaster, until the cheesecake pan is immersed halfway. Bake as directed. The extra moisture created with this method often prevents the cheesecake from cracking.

Death by Chocolate

YIELD: 15 SERVINGS

A dessert for the die-hard chocolate fan. Funny it was submitted by someone who is allergic to chocolate—she does not know what she is missing.

1 (22-ounce) package brownie mix	5 large Heath bars
1/3 cup Kahlúa	16 ounces whipped topping
3 envelopes chocolate mousse mix	

Bake the brownies using the package directions for a 9×13-inch baking pan. Pour the Kahlúa over the hot brownies. Let stand until cool. Cut into bars.

Prepare the mousse mix using the package directions. Crush the candy in a large sealable plastic food storage bag with a rolling pin.

Layer the brownies, mousse, whipped topping and candy 1/2 at a time in a large deep serving dish. Chill, covered, for 8 to 12 hours.

Becky Bennett
Vera Bradley Product Development Team

Chocolate Mousse Cake

YIELD: 15 SERVINGS

4 (3-ounce) packages ladyfingers, split lengthwise	1/3 cup water
	1 teaspoon vanilla extract
3 cups semisweet chocolate chips	8 eggs, separated
1 cup sugar	Confectioners' sugar

Line the bottom and side of a 9-inch springform pan with some of the ladyfingers split side in. Combine the chocolate chips, sugar and water in a medium saucepan. Cook over low heat until the chocolate is melted, stirring constantly. Remove from heat. Add the vanilla. Beat until smooth with a wooden spoon. Let cool slightly.

Beat the egg yolks at medium speed in a large mixing bowl. Add the chocolate mixture gradually, beating constantly. Continue beating until the mixture thickens.

Beat the egg whites in a mixing bowl until stiff peaks form. Fold into the chocolate mixture.

Spread 1/4 of the chocolate mixture in the prepared pan. Cover with another layer of ladyfingers. Repeat layering 3 more times. Chill, covered, for 4 hours or until firm. Sprinkle with confectioners' sugar just before serving.

Joyce Neubauer
Vera Bradley Classic Steering Committee

"Better than Martha's"
Chocolate Waffles with Boysenberry Sauce

Michael is always trying to outdo Martha. We think he has
finally done it with these waffles.

1 cup flour	1/2 cup (1 stick) butter
1 cup baking cocoa	4 egg yolks
2 1/2 teaspoons baking powder	2 cups heavy cream
1/2 teaspoon baking soda	3 tablespoons vanilla extract
1/2 teaspoon salt	4 egg whites, stiffly beaten
1 cup sugar	Boysenberry Sauce (page 167)
8 ounces semisweet chocolate	Natural vanilla ice cream

Sift the flour, baking cocoa, baking powder, baking soda, salt and sugar into a
large bowl. Place the chocolate and butter in a heatproof bowl. Set over a
saucepan of barely simmering water. Heat until melted, stirring constantly.
Remove from heat. Whisk in the egg yolks, cream and vanilla. Stir into the
flour mixture. Fold in the stiffly beaten egg whites.

Ladle about 1/3 cup of the batter onto each section of a preheated waffle
iron, spreading the batter almost to the edges. Close the lid. Bake on the lowest
heat setting for 3 1/2 to 4 minutes or until no steam emerges. Remove the waffles
and keep warm in the oven. Repeat the process with the remaining batter.

To serve, drizzle Boysenberry Sauce into designs of choice on individual
dessert plates. Arrange 1 waffle on each plate. Top with a small scoop of natural
vanilla ice cream. (If you were truly Martha Stewart, you would milk your own
Guernsey and churn your own.) Drizzle remaining Boysenberry Sauce over the
ice cream. Garnish with mint and fresh berries. (Martha would grow her own
berries . . . from seeds . . . grown from century-old plants . . . on an estate in
Provence.)

Boysenberry Sauce

YIELD: 1 CUP

2 pints fresh boysenberries or
  raspberries, puréed
1 ounce (or more) kirsch

2 tablespoons fresh lemon juice
1/4 cup honey

Strain the berries and remove the seeds individually with tweezers. Sample the kirsch. Go into your garden or conservatory and harvest 1 lemon. Squeeze the juice. Sample the kirsch again. Add 2 tablespoons lemon juice to the berries. Strain 1/4 cup honey from the comb gathered from your apiary over the berries. Add 1 ounce kirsch and blend until smooth.

Michael Nelaborige
Vera Bradley Marketing Assistant

Chocolate and Peanut Butter Dessert

YIELD: 15 SERVINGS

This is a terrific dish to take to a block party or large gathering—both kids and adults love it.

1 1/4 cups flour
2 tablespoons sugar
1/2 cup (1 stick) butter or margarine
2 cups peanut butter

1 1/2 cups confectioners' sugar
2 (4-ounce) packages chocolate
  instant pudding mix
16 ounces whipped topping

Mix the flour and sugar in a large bowl. Cut in the butter until crumbly. Pat over the bottom of a 9×13-inch baking pan. Bake at 350 degrees for 10 to 12 minutes or until golden brown. Combine the peanut butter and confectioners' sugar in a bowl and mix well. Crumble over the hot crust.

Prepare the pudding mix using the package directions. Spread over the peanut butter mixture. Top with the whipped topping. Chill, covered, for 8 to 12 hours. Serve at room temperature.

LeAnn Frankle
Vera Bradley Accounting Team

Kimberly's Pumpkin Cake Dessert

This recipe is best when made one day ahead.

1 (2-layer) package pudding-recipe
  yellow cake mix
1 egg
1/2 cup (1 stick) butter, melted
1 (16-ounce) can pumpkin
1/2 cup packed brown sugar

1/4 cup sugar
1 1/2 tablespoons cinnamon
1 (5-ounce) can evaporated milk
1/2 cup sugar
1/4 cup (1/2 stick) butter, softened
1 cup pecan pieces

Reserve 1 cup of the cake mix. Combine the remaining cake mix, egg and 1/2 cup butter in a mixing bowl and mix well. Spread over the bottom of a greased 9×13-inch baking pan.

Beat the pumpkin, brown sugar, 1/4 cup sugar, cinnamon and evaporated milk in a mixing bowl. Pour into the prepared pan.

Mix the reserved cake mix and 1/2 cup sugar in a bowl. Cut in 1/4 cup butter until crumbly. Sprinkle over the pumpkin layer. Sprinkle with pecans. Bake at 350 degrees for 1 hour. Let stand until cool. Chill, covered, in the refrigerator.

Vi MacMurdo
Lady Vi
Volant, Pennsylvania

Layered Mocha Cream Torte

2¹/2 cups ground chocolate wafer
  cookies or chocolate graham
  crackers
1¹/2 tablespoons instant coffee
6 tablespoons butter, melted
12 ounces semisweet chocolate,
  chopped
6 tablespoons unsalted butter, chopped

1 teaspoon instant coffee
¹/2 cup sugar
3 tablespoons water
5 egg whites
5 teaspoons instant coffee
2³/4 cups chilled whipping cream
¹/4 cup confectioners' sugar
¹/4 teaspoon cinnamon

Process the ground cookies and 1¹/2 tablespoons coffee powder in a food
processor. Reserve ³/4 cup of the mixture for the topping. Add 6 tablespoons
butter to the remaining crumb mixture and process until moist. Press over the
bottom and up the side of a 9-inch springform pan. Bake at 350 degrees for
10 minutes or until firm to the touch. Cool completely.

Combine the chocolate, 6 tablespoons unsalted butter and 1 teaspoon
coffee powder in a heavy medium saucepan. Cook over low heat until
melted and smooth, stirring constantly. Pour into a large mixing bowl. Cool
to lukewarm.

Heat ¹/2 cup sugar and water in a small saucepan over low heat until the
sugar dissolves. Increase the heat. Boil for 4 minutes or until a candy
thermometer registers 240 degrees; do not stir.

Beat the egg whites in a large mixing bowl until soft peaks form, using
chilled beaters. Add the hot syrup gradually, beating constantly. Continue
beating for 3 minutes or until medium-stiff peaks form. Fold ¹/3 of the meringue
into the lukewarm chocolate mixture to lighten. Fold in the remaining
meringue.

Dissolve 5 teaspoons coffee powder in ¹/4 cup of the cream in a large bowl.
Add the remaining 2¹/2 cups cream, confectioners' sugar and cinnamon. Beat
until stiff peaks form. Fold 1¹/2 cups of the coffee whipped cream into the
chocolate meringue, forming mocha mousse.

Spoon ¹/2 of the mocha mousse over the crust. Sprinkle 3 tablespoons of
the reserved crumb mixture over the mousse. Spoon ¹/2 of the remaining coffee
whipped cream over the crumbs. Sprinkle with 3 tablespoons of the remaining
crumb mixture. Repeat layering with the remaining mocha mousse, crumbs and
coffee whipped cream, ending with the crumbs. Chill, covered, for 4 hours or
until set. Run a knife around the edge to loosen from the pan. Remove the side
of the pan and serve. You may prepare up to 2 days in advance.

Stacey Sloan Brown
Friend of Vera Bradley Designs

All-American Peppermint Stick Torte with Fudge Topping

YIELD: 15 SERVINGS

This is time consuming, but it is delicious and makes
a beautiful holiday dessert.

1 (9-ounce) package chocolate
  wafers, crushed
2 tablespoons sugar
1/2 cup (1 stick) unsalted butter or
  margarine, melted, cooled
1 (7-ounce) package hard red and
  white striped peppermint candies
  (about 45 pieces)
6 egg yolks

1/2 cup sugar
1/4 cup water
1/2 teaspoon peppermint extract
5 cups whipping cream
1/2 cup dark corn syrup
12 ounces bittersweet or semisweet
  chocolate, chopped
Peppermint candies

Process the wafers and 2 tablespoons sugar in a food processor until ground. Add the butter and process until blended. Press over the bottom and up the side of a 9-inch springform pan. Freeze until firm.

Process the candies in a food processor until ground, leaving some small pieces. Whisk the egg yolks, 1/2 cup sugar and water in a medium metal bowl until blended. Set over a saucepan of rapidly simmering water; do not allow the bottom of the bowl to touch the water. Cook for 6 minutes or until a candy thermometer registers 170 degrees, whisking constantly. Remove the bowl from over the water. Add 1/2 of the ground candy and whisk until melted. Let stand for 5 minutes or until cool, whisking occasionally. Stir in the remaining ground candy and peppermint extract. Beat 3 cups of the whipping cream in a mixing bowl until stiff peaks form. Fold into the candy mixture. Spoon into the frozen crust, smoothing the top. Freeze, covered, for 6 to 12 hours or until firm.

Bring 1 cup of the remaining whipping cream and corn syrup to a simmer in a heavy medium saucepan. Remove from heat. Add the chocolate and whisk until smooth. Cool for 30 minutes or until barely lukewarm and slightly thickened, whisking occasionally.

Spoon 1 cup of the chocolate sauce over the frozen filling, spreading to the edge. Freeze, covered, for 2 hours or until firm. Reheat the remaining chocolate sauce in a saucepan over low heat, stirring frequently. Run a sharp knife around the edge of the pan to loosen. Release the side of the pan. Place the torte on a dessert platter.

Beat the remaining 1 cup whipping cream in a large bowl until stiff peaks form. Spoon into a pastry bag fitted with a star tip. Pipe rosettes of whipped cream around the top of the torte. Place peppermint candies between the rosettes. Serve with the warm chocolate sauce.

Leslie K. Byrne
Daughter-in-law of Barbara Bradley Baekgaard

Éclair Torte

*I'm not known for my extravagant desserts, but this
one impressed 'em all!*

1 cup water
1/2 cup (1 stick) butter
1/4 teaspoon salt
1 cup flour
4 eggs
8 ounces cream cheese, softened

2 (4-ounce) packages vanilla instant
   pudding mix
3 cups milk
2 cups whipped topping
Chocolate sauce

Bring the water, butter and salt to a boil in a large saucepan. Add the flour and
stir with a wooden spoon to form a smooth ball. Remove from heat. Add the
eggs 1 at a time, beating well after each addition. Spread the batter in a greased
9×13-inch baking pan. Bake at 400 degrees for 25 to 30 minutes or until golden
brown. Cool on a wire rack.

    Beat the cream cheese in a mixing bowl until smooth. Add the pudding
mix and milk and beat until smooth. Spread over the crust. Chill, covered, for
30 minutes. Uncover and spread whipped topping over the top. Drizzle with
chocolate sauce. Do not substitute margarine for the butter in this recipe.

LeAnn Frankle
Vera Bradley Accounting Team

Strawberry Custard

YIELD: 6 SERVINGS

1 pint strawberries, hulled, quartered
2 egg yolks
3 eggs
1/2 cup sugar

1/8 teaspoon salt
3 cups very hot milk
1 1/2 teaspoons vanilla extract

Place the strawberries in 6 buttered ramekins. Beat the egg yolks and eggs in a mixing bowl until blended. Stir in the sugar and salt. Add the hot milk gradually, stirring constantly. Stir in the vanilla. Pour over the strawberries. Place the ramekins in a large baking dish. Add enough water to the larger dish to come 1/2 way up the side of the ramekins. Bake at 325 degrees for 30 minutes. Remove the ramekins to a wire rack to cool. Garnish with fruit and confectioners' sugar. Serve each with a fancy cookie.

A. Kay Black
The Blackboard
Jacksonville, Illinois

Walloon Lake Inn's
Grand Marnier Sabayon Sauce

YIELD: ABOUT 2 CUPS

4 egg yolks
1/3 cup sugar
3 tablespoons Grand Marnier or other
   orange-flavor liqueur

1 cup whipping cream
Sliced fresh strawberries or other
   fresh fruit

Beat the egg yolks, sugar and Grand Marnier in a medium saucepan. Cook over medium-low heat for 12 minutes or until thickened to the consistency of thin batter. Remove from heat. Chill, covered, for 2 hours or longer.
   Beat the whipping cream in a chilled mixing bowl until stiff peaks form. Fold in the chilled egg mixture. Serve over sliced strawberries.

Mary Ann Gray
Vera Bradley Sales Representative

Aunt Franny's Apple Cake

YIELD: 16 SERVINGS

This is a great breakfast or afternoon tea cake.

5 tablespoons sugar
2 teaspoons ground cinnamon
1 teaspoon ground nutmeg
5 eggs
2 cups sugar
1 cup vegetable oil

1/4 cup orange juice
3 cups flour
1 tablespoon baking powder
2 1/2 teaspoons vanilla extract
6 or 7 medium apples, peeled, sliced
Brandy Glaze (below)

Mix 5 tablespoons sugar, cinnamon and nutmeg in a small bowl. Beat the eggs, 2 cups sugar, oil and orange juice in a mixing bowl. Add the flour, baking powder and vanilla and beat until smooth.

Spoon 1/3 of the batter into a buttered bundt pan. Arrange a layer of apples over the batter. Sprinkle with 1/2 of the cinnamon mixture. Repeat layers with the remaining batter, apples and cinnamon mixture. Bake at 350 degrees for 1 1/2 hours. Remove from the oven and pierce the cake with a fork. Pour Brandy Glaze over the cake. Cool on a wire rack. Invert onto a cake plate and serve.

Brandy Glaze

YIELD: 3 TABLESPOONS

1 tablespoon margarine
1 tablespoon confectioners' sugar

1 tablespoon brandy

Melt the margarine in a saucepan over low heat. Add the confectioners' sugar and brandy and stir until smooth.

Stefanie Chevillet
Vera Bradley Customer Service

For a fun spring party, try a "Bunny Nibble." Use your garden, or create one with potted plants or bouquets of fresh herbs and flowers. Try English ivy and moss as table accents. Serve fresh vegetable dishes in unusual ways: Artichoke Phyllo Flowers (page 44) can bloom on a platter covered in Italian parsley and edible violets. Create a large red pepper "bowl" for Millie's Curried Dip (page 38) served with fresh vegetables (try exotic varieties). Present a Tomato Pesto Cheese Mold (page 34) with warm dill bread baguettes on a glazed terra cotta saucer. Of course, don't forget the carrot cake! Use partyware decorated with Peter Rabbit illustrations. Be the original organic host!

Traditional Carrot Cake

YIELD: 16 SERVINGS

This is a tried-and-true favorite.

2 cups flour
2 teaspoons baking soda
2 teaspoons cinnamon
1 teaspoon salt
2 cups sugar
1 1/2 cups vegetable oil

2 teaspoons vanilla extract
4 eggs
3 cups shredded carrots
1/2 cup chopped walnuts
Cream Cheese Frosting (below)

Sift the flour, baking soda, cinnamon and salt together. Combine the sugar, oil, vanilla and 1/2 of the flour mixture in a bowl and whisk well. Add the remaining flour mixture alternately with the eggs and carrots, stirring well after each addition. Fold in the walnuts. Pour into a nonstick tube or bundt pan. Bake at 350 degrees for 40 to 45 minutes or until a wooden pick inserted in the center comes out clean. Cool in the pan on a wire rack. Invert the cake onto a cake plate. Frost with Cream Cheese Frosting.

Cream Cheese Frosting

YIELD: 16 SERVINGS

8 ounces cream cheese, softened
1/2 cup (1 stick) butter or margarine, softened

1 teaspoon vanilla extract
2 cups confectioners' sugar

Beat the cream cheese and butter in a mixing bowl until light and fluffy. Add the vanilla and confectioners' sugar and beat until smooth.

Joan Bradley Reedy
Vera Bradley Sales Representative
Daughter of Vera Bradley

Chiffon Cake with Citrus Sauce

YIELD: 12 TO 16 SERVINGS

In a hurry? May we suggest a purchased angel food cake
served with the Citrus Sauce? Your guests will never know.

1 package angel food cake mix	1/4 cup flour
1 cup water	2 tablespoons lemon zest
3/4 cup vegetable oil	1/2 teaspoon vanilla extract
3 eggs	Citrus Sauce (below)

Combine the egg white packet from the cake mix and the water in a large
mixing bowl. Beat at low speed for 1 minute. Beat at high speed until stiff
peaks form.

Combine the flour mixture from the cake mix, oil, eggs, 1/4 cup flour, lemon
zest and vanilla in a large mixing bowl. Beat at low speed until blended. Beat at
medium speed for 3 minutes. Fold in the beaten egg white mixture. Pour into
an ungreased 10-inch tube pan. Run a knife through the batter to remove air
bubbles. Bake at 350 degrees for 40 to 45 minutes or until a wooden pick
inserted in the center comes out clean. Cool on a wire rack.

To serve, cut the cake into slices and place on individual dessert plates.
Spoon Citrus Sauce over the cake. Garnish with sliced strawberries, blueberries
and sliced kiwifruit.

Citrus Sauce

YIELD: 12 TO 16 SERVINGS

1 cup sugar	1 tablespoon lemon juice
1/3 cup orange juice	1 teaspoon lemon zest
1 egg, lightly beaten	1 cup whipping cream, whipped

Combine the sugar, orange juice, egg, lemon juice and lemon zest in a heavy
saucepan. Cook over medium heat for 10 minutes or until the mixture comes to
a boil, stirring constantly. Remove from heat. Chill in the refrigerator. Fold in
the whipped cream.

Nancy Graham
Vera Bradley Customer Service–Retired

Nectarine Coconut Cake

A summertime favorite of Sue's family and Vera Bradley Designs.

2 eggs
$^1/_2$ cup vegetable oil
$^2/_3$ cup honey
$^3/_4$ cup plain yogurt
1 teaspoon vanilla extract

2 cups cake flour
1 teaspoon baking soda
1 cup shredded coconut
1$^1/_2$ cups fresh nectarine sections
6 tablespoons cinnamon

Beat the eggs in a mixing bowl until pale yellow. Add the oil, honey, yogurt and vanilla. Add the cake flour and baking soda, stirring to mix well. Stir in the coconut.

Pour $^1/_4$ of the batter into a greased 6-cup tube pan. Arrange $^1/_3$ of the nectarines evenly over the batter. Sprinkle with 2 tablespoons of the cinnamon. Repeat the layers twice, ending with the batter. Bake at 350 degrees for 40 to 45 minutes or until the cake tests done. Store in the refrigerator.

Sue Britton
Vera Bradley Marketing Manager

Chocolate Mint Squares

YIELD: 24 SERVINGS

This is one recipe that I have called on over the years for numerous occasions . . . from birthdays to carry-ins. I like this cake because it's so rich and moist. Don't be surprised if someone asks for the recipe . . . it's that good!

1 cup (2 sticks) butter or margarine, softened
1 cup sugar
4 eggs, lightly beaten
1 (16-ounce) can chocolate syrup
1 teaspoon vanilla extract
1 cup flour

1/2 teaspoon salt
1/2 cup (1 stick) butter or margarine, softened
2 cups confectioners' sugar
2 tablespoons crème de menthe
Chocolate Glaze (below)

Beat 1 cup butter and sugar in a large mixing bowl until light and fluffy. Add the eggs, chocolate syrup and vanilla and beat well. Add the flour and salt and beat until smooth. Pour into a greased 9×13-inch cake pan. Bake at 350 degrees for 30 minutes or until a wooden pick inserted in the center comes out clean. Remove to a wire rack to cool.

Cream 1/2 cup butter and confectioners' sugar in a mixing bowl. Add the crème de menthe and beat well. Spread over the cool cake. Spread Chocolate Glaze over the top. Chill, covered, for 6 hours or longer. Cut into squares.

Chocolate Glaze

YIELD: 24 SERVINGS

1 cup chocolate chips

6 tablespoons butter or margarine

Melt the chocolate chips and butter in a small saucepan, stirring frequently. Remove from heat and cool slightly.

Diane Brown
Vera Bradley Shipping Team

Triple-Chocolate Layer Cake

$^1/_2$ cup cold buttermilk
1 tablespoon instant espresso powder
2 teaspoons vanilla extract
$1^1/_4$ cups sugar
1 cup cake flour
6 tablespoons baking cocoa
$^1/_2$ teaspoon salt
$^1/_4$ teaspoon baking soda
$^1/_4$ teaspoon baking powder
3 eggs

$^1/_2$ cup (1 stick) unsalted butter, softened
4 ounces white chocolate, finely chopped
4 ounces milk chocolate, finely chopped
1 cup plus 1 tablespoon heavy cream
6 ounces semisweet chocolate, finely chopped

Butter three 8-inch round cake pans. Line the bottom of the pans with parchment paper. Combine the buttermilk, espresso powder and vanilla in a small bowl and stir until the espresso powder dissolves.

Sift the sugar, cake flour, baking cocoa, salt, baking soda and baking powder into a large mixing bowl. Add the eggs and butter and beat until thick and smooth. Add the buttermilk mixture. Beat for $1^1/_2$ minutes or until light and fluffy. Pour into the prepared pans.

Bake at 350 degrees for 20 minutes or until a tester inserted in the center comes out clean. Cool in the pans on wire racks for 5 minutes. Invert the layers onto the wire racks and remove the parchment paper. Let stand until cooled completely.

Place the chopped white chocolate and chopped milk chocolate in separate medium mixing bowls. Bring 1 cup of the cream to a boil in a heavy medium saucepan. Pour 3 tablespoons of the hot cream over the white chocolate and stir until smooth. Pour 3 tablespoons of the hot cream over the milk chocolate and stir until smooth. Chill both mixtures for 15 minutes.

Add the semisweet chocolate to the remaining hot cream in the saucepan and stir until smooth.

Place 1 cake layer on a cake plate. Beat the white chocolate filling until slightly stiff. Spread over the cake layer. Top with the second cake layer. Add the remaining 1 tablespoon cream to the milk chocolate filling and beat until smooth. Spread over the second cake layer. Top with the third cake layer. Chill for 30 minutes or until the semisweet chocolate frosting is firm enough to spread.

Stir the frosting until smooth. Spread a very thin layer over the top and side of the cake to smooth the surface. Chill for 30 minutes. Spread the remaining frosting decoratively over the top and side of cake. Garnish with white chocolate and milk chocolate shavings.

Amy Ray
Granddaughter of Vera Bradley

Bourbon Chocolate Pecan Cake

YIELD: 12 SERVINGS

2 cups pecan halves
1 cup (2 sticks) unsalted butter
8 ounces bittersweet or semisweet
  chocolate
1 1/2 cups sugar

1 cup baking cocoa
6 eggs
1/3 cup bourbon
Chocolate Glaze (below)

Spread the pecans on a baking sheet. Bake at 350 degrees for 10 minutes or until toasted and fragrant. Remove from the oven and cool. Chop the pecans coarsely.

Cut a circle of parchment paper to fit the bottom of a 9-inch round cake pan. Butter the cake pan well and line with the parchment paper, making sure the parchment paper lies flat.

Melt the butter and chocolate in a double boiler over simmering water, stirring frequently. Let stand until cool.

Combine the sugar, baking cocoa and eggs in a large bowl and mix well. Stir in the melted chocolate. Stir in 1 1/2 cups of the pecans. Stir in the bourbon.

Pour into the prepared cake pan. Place the cake pan inside a larger pan. Pour enough hot water into the larger pan to come 1 inch up the side of the smaller pan. Bake for 45 minutes or until the cake is firm to the touch. The surface may crack a little. Cool the cake on a wire rack. Remove the cake from the pan, leaving the parchment paper attached. Wrap in plastic wrap. Chill for 8 to 12 hours.

Unwrap the cake. Invert onto a wire rack over a sheet of waxed paper. Peel off the parchment paper. Drizzle spoonfuls of Chocolate Glaze along the edge of the cake so that it drips down and coats the side. Spoon Chocolate Glaze over the top of the cake and smooth with a rubber spatula. Cover the side of the cake with the remaining chopped pecans by pressing gently against the side. Chill, covered, until 30 minutes before serving.

Chocolate Glaze

YIELD: 12 SERVINGS

4 ounces bittersweet or semisweet
  chocolate

1/2 cup (1 stick) unsalted butter

Melt the chocolate and butter in a double boiler over simmering water, stirring until smooth. Remove from heat. Cool for 5 minutes.

Debbie Peterson
Vera Bradley Classic Steering Committee

Hummingbird Cake

3 cups flour
2 cups sugar
1 teaspoon baking soda
1 teaspoon salt
1 teaspoon cinnamon
3 eggs, lightly beaten
3/4 cup vegetable oil

1 1/2 teaspoons vanilla extract
1 cup pecans, chopped
2 cups sliced bananas
1 (8-ounce) can crushed pineapple,
  drained
Cream Cheese Frosting (below)

Sift the flour, sugar, baking soda, salt and cinnamon into a large mixing bowl. Add the eggs, oil and vanilla and mix well. Stir in the pecans, bananas and pineapple.

Pour into a greased and floured tube pan. Bake at 325 degrees for 1 1/4 hours. Cool in the pan on a wire rack. Invert onto a cake plate. Frost with Cream Cheese Frosting.

Cream Cheese Frosting

8 ounces cream cheese, softened
1/2 cup (1 stick) butter, softened
1 (1-pound) package confectioners'
  sugar

1 teaspoon vanilla extract

Beat the cream cheese and butter in a mixing bowl until light and fluffy. Add the confectioners' sugar and vanilla and beat until smooth. Do not use light butter in this recipe.

Mercedes Cox
Friend of Vera Bradley Designs

Orange Blossom Bridesmaid Luncheon Cake

YIELD: 16 SERVINGS

This is a beautiful cake to serve at any luncheon.

1¹/₂ cups flour
1¹/₂ teaspoons baking powder
¹/₄ teaspoon salt
1 cup (2 sticks) butter or margarine,
  softened
1 cup sugar
1 tablespoon orange zest

2 eggs
¹/₂ cup orange juice
1 tablespoon orange liqueur
1 teaspoon lemon juice
¹/₂ teaspoon vanilla extract
Candied Orange Peel (below)

Mix the flour, baking powder and salt in a bowl. Beat the butter at medium speed in a mixing bowl until creamy, scraping the bowl occasionally. Add 1 cup sugar gradually, beating constantly for 5 to 7 minutes or until light and fluffy. Add the orange zest and eggs 1 at a time, beating just until blended after each addition.

Add the flour mixture alternately with the orange juice, beating constantly at low speed until blended after each addition and beginning and ending with the flour mixture. Stir in the liqueur, lemon juice and vanilla.

Spoon the batter into a greased and floured 6-cup bundt pan. Bake at 350 degrees for 35 to 40 minutes or until a wooden pick inserted in the center comes out clean. Cool in the pan on a wire rack for 10 minutes. Invert onto the wire rack to cool completely. Sprinkle Candied Orange Peel over the cooled cake.

Candied Orange Peel

YIELD: 16 SERVINGS

1 large orange
3 tablespoons light corn syrup

¹/₄ cup sugar

Peel the orange and cut into ¹/₈-inch strips. Reserve the orange sections for another use. Combine the peel and corn syrup in a saucepan. Bring to a boil over medium heat; reduce heat. Cook for 3 to 4 minutes, stirring frequently. Combine the peel with ¹/₄ cup sugar in a bowl and toss to coat. Spread in a single layer on waxed paper. Let stand until dry.

Patricia R. Miller
President and Co-Founder of Vera Bradley

Pecan Pie Cake

....

YIELD: 12 TO 16 SERVINGS

To make the assembly of the cake easier, prepare the pecan pie
filling and the pastry garnish the day before serving.

3 cups finely chopped pecans, toasted

1/2 cup (1 stick) butter or margarine,
    softened

1/2 cup shortening

2 cups sugar

5 egg yolks

1 tablespoon vanilla extract

2 cups flour

1 teaspoon baking soda

1 cup buttermilk

5 egg whites

3/4 cup dark corn syrup

Pecan Pie Cake Filling (page 183)

Pastry Leaves and Pecans (page 183)

Sprinkle 2 cups of the pecans evenly into 3 greased 9-inch round cake pans.
Shake to coat the bottoms of the pans.

Beat the butter and shortening at medium speed in a mixing bowl until
fluffy. Add the sugar gradually, beating constantly. Add the egg yolks 1 at a
time, beating until blended after each addition. Stir in the vanilla. Add the
flour and baking soda alternately with the buttermilk, beginning and ending
with the flour and beating at low speed until blended after each addition. Stir
in the remaining 1 cup chopped pecans.

Beat the egg whites at medium speed in a mixing bowl until stiff peaks
form. Fold 1/3 of the beaten egg whites into the batter. Fold in the remaining
beaten egg whites. Pour into the prepared pans.

Bake at 350 degrees for 25 to 30 minutes or until the layers test done,
covering with foil if the layers are browning too quickly. Cool in the pans for
10 minutes. Invert onto wire racks lined with waxed paper. Brush the top and
side of the layers with corn syrup. Let stand to cool completely.

To assemble, place 1 cake layer pecan side up on a cake platter. Spread with
1/2 of the Pecan Pie Cake Filling. Place the second cake layer pecan side up on
top of the first layer. Spoon the remaining Pecan Pie Cake Filling over the top
and spread evenly. Top with the remaining cake layer pecan side up. Garnish
with Pastry Leaves and Pecans.

Pecan Pie Cake Filling

YIELD: 12 TO 16 SERVINGS

1/2 cup packed brown sugar

3/4 cup dark corn syrup

1/3 cup cornstarch

4 egg yolks

1 1/2 cups half-and-half

1/8 teaspoon salt

3 tablespoons butter or margarine

1 teaspoon vanilla extract

Combine the brown sugar, corn syrup, cornstarch, egg yolks, half-and-half and salt in a heavy medium saucepan and whisk until smooth. Bring to a boil over medium heat, whisking constantly. Boil for 1 minute or until thickened, whisking constantly. Remove from heat. Whisk in the butter and vanilla. Pour into a large glass bowl. Place a sheet of waxed paper directly on the surface. Cover with plastic wrap. Chill for 4 hours or longer. You may prepare and refrigerate for up to 2 days before using.

Pastry Leaves and Pecans

YIELD: 12 TO 16 SERVINGS

2 refrigerated pie pastries

24 pecan halves

1 egg

1 tablespoon water

Sugar

Unfold the pastries and press out the fold lines. Cut 8 to 10 leaves out of each pastry with a 3-inch leaf-shape cookie cutter; mark the veins using the tip of a knife.

Crumble 10 to 12 small pieces of foil into 1/2-inch balls. Coat with nonstick cooking spray and place on a lightly greased baking sheet. Drape a pastry leaf over each ball; place the remaining pastry leaves directly on the baking sheet.

Pinch 12 pea-size pieces from pastry trimmings and shape into small balls. Cut twelve 2-inch pieces of pastry from the trimmings. Sandwich 1 pastry ball between 2 pecan halves. Wrap the bottom portion with a 2-inch piece of pastry to resemble half-shelled pecans. Repeat the process with the remaining pecans and pastry. Place on the baking sheet with the pastry leaves.

Whisk the egg and water in a small bowl. Brush over the leaves and the pecans. Sprinkle with sugar. Bake at 350 degrees for 6 to 8 minutes. Cool on a wire rack. Store in an airtight container until ready to assemble the cake.

Stefanie Chevillet
Vera Bradley Customer Service

Pumpkin Roll with Toffee Cream Filling and Caramel Sauce

3/4 cup flour
1 1/2 teaspoons cinnamon
1 1/4 teaspoons ginger
3/4 teaspoon allspice
6 egg yolks
1/3 cup sugar
1/3 cup packed brown sugar
2/3 cup canned solid-pack pumpkin

6 egg whites
1/8 teaspoon salt
Confectioners' sugar
1/4 cup English toffee pieces
Toffee Cream Filling (page 185)
1 1/2 cups prepared caramel sauce, warmed
1/4 cup English toffee pieces

Sift the flour, cinnamon, ginger and allspice into a small bowl. Beat the egg yolks, sugar and brown sugar in a large mixing bowl for 3 minutes or until very thick. Beat in the pumpkin at low speed. Add the flour mixture and beat until smooth.

Beat the egg whites with the salt in a mixing bowl until stiff peaks form. Fold 1/3 at a time into the batter. Pour into a jelly roll pan sprayed with nonstick cooking spray. Bake at 375 degrees for 15 minutes or until a tester inserted in the center comes out clean.

Place a smooth kitchen towel on a work surface. Dust generously with confectioners' sugar. Run a knife around the edges of the pan to loosen the cake. Invert the cake onto the towel. Fold the towel over 1 long side of the cake. Roll up the cake in the towel. Let stand seam side down for 1 hour or until cool.

Unroll the cake. Sprinkle with 1/4 cup toffee pieces. Spread with Toffee Cream Filling. Roll up the cake loosely to enclose the filling, beginning at the long side and using the towel as an aid. Place seam side down on a cake plate. You may prepare 1 day ahead and chill, covered, in the refrigerator.

To serve, trim the ends of the cake roll on a slight diagonal. Sprinkle with confectioners' sugar. Spoon some of the warm caramel sauce over the top. Sprinkle with 1/4 cup toffee pieces. Cut into slices 1 inch thick and place on individual dessert plates. Serve with the remaining caramel sauce.

Toffee Cream Filling

YIELD: 8 TO 12 SERVINGS

1 teaspoon unflavored gelatin
2 tablespoons dark rum
1 cup whipping cream, chilled

3 tablespoons confectioners' sugar
1/2 cup English toffee pieces

Sprinkle the gelatin over 2 tablespoons rum in a small heavy saucepan. Let stand for 10 minutes or until softened. Cook over low heat until the gelatin dissolves. Beat the whipping cream and confectioners' sugar in a mixing bowl until stiff peaks form. Beat in the gelatin mixture. Fold in the toffee pieces.

Stefanie Chevillet
Vera Bradley Customer Service

Ruth's Italian Pound Cake

YIELD: 16 SERVINGS

When I was very pregnant with my third child, we went to a party where this was served. I consumed at least *half* of the cake. The next day Henry was born. As a "welcome home" gift, Ruth baked another cake for me and attached the recipe. Serve this with dinner, and the leftovers (if any) are great for breakfast.

3/4 cup butter, softened
3 cups sugar
3/4 cup vegetable oil
1 cup milk

6 eggs
3 cups flour
1 tablespoon baking powder
2 teaspoons almond extract

Beat the butter in a mixing bowl until light and fluffy. Add the sugar gradually, beating constantly. Beat in the oil and milk. Add the eggs 1 at a time, beating well after each addition. Beat in the flour, baking powder and almond flavoring. Pour into a greased and floured bundt pan. Bake at 325 degrees for 90 minutes.

Joanie Byrne Hall
Granddaughter of Vera Bradley

Sloppy Pineapple Cake

2 cups flour
2 cups sugar
2 teaspoons baking soda
2 eggs
1 teaspoon vanilla extract

1 (8-ounce) can juice-pack crushed
  pineapple
1/2 cup pecans, chopped
Pecan Cream Cheese Frosting
  (below)

Mix the flour, sugar and baking soda in a mixing bowl. Add the eggs and vanilla and beat well. Stir in the undrained pineapple and pecans. Pour into a nonstick 9×13-inch cake pan.

Bake at 350 degrees for 30 to 40 minutes or until the cake tests done. Spread Pecan Cream Cheese Frosting over the cake while still warm.

Pecan Cream Cheese Frosting

8 ounces cream cheese, softened
1/2 cup (1 stick) butter, softened
2 cups confectioners' sugar

1 teaspoon vanilla extract
1/2 cup crushed pecans

Beat the cream cheese and butter in a mixing bowl until light and fluffy. Add the confectioners' sugar and vanilla and beat until smooth. Stir in the pecans.

Sandy Schelm
Rustic Hutch
Fort Wayne, Indiana

Vera's Yum-Yum Cake

YIELD: 15 SERVINGS

Vera served this cake for all of her grandchildren's
birthdays—and they still love it to this day.

1 (2-layer) package yellow cake mix
8 ounces cream cheese, softened
1 (4-ounce) package vanilla instant
    pudding mix
1 cup milk
16 ounces whipped topping

2 (16-ounce) packages fresh
    strawberries or frozen strawberries,
    thawed
2 cups shredded coconut
1 cup chopped walnuts

Prepare and bake the cake using the package directions for a 9×13-inch cake
pan and baking for 20 to 22 minutes. Cool in the pan on a wire rack.

Beat the cream cheese in a mixing bowl until light and fluffy. Add the
pudding mix and milk and beat until smooth. Fold in the whipped topping.
Spread over the cooled cake. Arrange the strawberries evenly over the
cake. Sprinkle with the coconut and walnuts. Chill, covered, for 4 to 6 hours
before serving.

Barbara Bradley Baekgaard
President and Co-Founder of Vera Bradley

Vanilla Butter and Nut Cake

YIELD: 12 TO 16 SERVINGS

A beautiful triple-layer cake, this is the perfect ending to dinner with friends.

1 cup (2 sticks) margarine
2 cups sugar
1 teaspoon baking soda
1/4 teaspoon salt
1 cup buttermilk

3 cups flour, sifted
1 tablespoon butter and nut flavoring
3 eggs, separated
Butter and Nut Frosting (below)

Bring all ingredients to room temperature. Cream the margarine and sugar in a mixing bowl until light and fluffy. Add the baking soda and salt to the buttermilk and stir until foamy. Add to the creamed mixture alternately with the flour, beating well after each addition. Add the flavoring. Beat in the egg yolks 1 at a time. Whip the egg whites in a mixing bowl until frothy. Fold into the batter.

Pour into 3 round cake pans sprayed with nonstick cooking spray. Bake at 350 degrees for 30 minutes or until a tester inserted in the center comes out clean. Cool on wire racks.

Spread Butter and Nut Frosting between the layers and over the top and side of the cake.

Butter and Nut Frosting

YIELD: 12 TO 16 SERVINGS

8 ounces cream cheese, softened
1/2 cup (1 stick) butter, softened
1 (1-pound) package confectioners'
  sugar

1 tablespoon butter and nut flavoring
1 cup chopped pecans or walnuts

Beat the cream cheese and butter in a mixing bowl until light and fluffy. Add the confectioners' sugar and flavoring and beat until smooth. Stir in the pecans.

Jane Jarvis
The Jarvis Shoppe
Bradenton, Florida

Joel's Award-Winning Fudge

YIELD: 16 SERVINGS

This is my son Joel's award-winning fudge recipe. He is now sixteen
and has entered it in the county fair since he was five years old. Several
times he has won Grand Champion. At the fair the judges always
kid him that he needs to bring ice cream in case the fudge should melt
in the 100-degree temperature in August.

1 (16-ounce) package chocolate chips   2 teaspoons vanilla extract
1 (14-ounce) can sweetened
condensed milk

Combine the chocolate chips, condensed milk and vanilla in a large
microwave-safe bowl. Microwave on High until the chocolate chips are almost
melted. Remove from the microwave and stir until smooth. Pour into a greased
8×8-inch dish. Chill, covered, in the refrigerator until set. Cut into squares. You
may use 3 parts chocolate chips and 1 part peanut butter chips, raspberry-flavor
chips or coffee-flavor chips to vary the flavor of the fudge.

Mary Jo Hetrick
Good Scents, Ltd.
Princeton, Illinois

Praline Grahams

YIELD: 3 1/2 DOZEN

These are great with a cup of coffee.

1 (16-ounce) package graham   1/2 cup sugar
   crackers   3/4 cup pecans, chopped
1/2 to 3/4 cup butter

Separate the graham crackers. Arrange in an 11×15-inch baking pan with the
edges of the graham crackers touching. Melt the butter in a saucepan. Stir in
the sugar and pecans. Bring to a boil. Cook for 3 minutes, stirring frequently.
Spread over the graham crackers. Bake at 300 degrees for 12 minutes. Remove
from the pan and cool on waxed paper.

Betsy Lewis Harned
Betsy Anne's
Glasgow, Kentucky

Applesauce Jumbles

YIELD: 5 DOZEN

These jumbles are great! The Browned Butter Glaze makes them wonderful.

1/2 cup shortening	1 teaspoon cinnamon
2 eggs	1 teaspoon vanilla extract
2 3/4 cups flour	1/4 teaspoon ground cloves
1 1/2 cups packed brown sugar	1 cup raisins
1 teaspoon salt	1 cup nuts, chopped
1/2 teaspoon baking soda	Browned Butter Glaze (below)
3/4 cup applesauce	

Beat the shortening and eggs in a mixing bowl until light and fluffy. Add the flour, brown sugar, salt, baking soda, applesauce, cinnamon, vanilla and cloves and mix well. Stir in the raisins and nuts. Chill, covered, in the refrigerator if the dough is too soft.

Drop the dough by rounded teaspoonfuls about 2 inches apart on an ungreased cookie sheet. Bake at 375 degrees for 10 minutes or until almost no indentation remains when touched. Cool on a wire rack. Spread with the Browned Butter Glaze.

Browned Butter Glaze

YIELD: ENOUGH FOR 5 DOZEN

1/3 cup butter or margarine	1 1/2 teaspoons vanilla extract
2 cups confectioners' sugar	2 to 4 tablespoons hot water

Heat the butter in a saucepan over low heat until golden brown. Remove from heat. Add the confectioners' sugar and vanilla and mix well. Stir in enough of the hot water to form a smooth glaze consistency.

Sue Britton
Vera Bradley Marketing Manager

Cinnamon and Sugar Biscotti

YIELD: 2 DOZEN

This is a wonderful cookie to serve with your coffee after a meal
when you really don't feel like having a big dessert.

2 cups flour
1¹/2 teaspoons cinnamon
1 teaspoon baking powder
¹/4 teaspoon salt
1 cup sugar
6 tablespoons unsalted butter, softened

1 egg
1 teaspoon vanilla extract
1 egg
3 tablespoons sugar
1 teaspoon cinnamon

Line 2 large cookie sheets with parchment paper. Mix the flour, 1¹/2 teaspoons
cinnamon, baking powder and salt in a medium bowl. Beat 1 cup sugar and
butter in a large mixing bowl until fluffy. Add 1 egg and beat well. Add the
vanilla and flour mixture and beat until thoroughly incorporated.

Divide the dough into 2 equal portions. Shape each portion into a 9-inch
log. Place on the prepared cookie sheets. Beat 1 egg in a small bowl. Brush the
logs with the beaten egg. Bake at 325 degrees for 50 minutes or until golden
brown and firm to the touch. The dough will spread. Cool on the cookie sheets.

Mix 3 tablespoons sugar and 1 teaspoon cinnamon in a bowl. Cut the logs
into diagonal slices ¹/2 inch wide. Place cut side down on the cookie sheets.
Sprinkle ¹/4 teaspoon of the cinnamon-sugar over each. Bake for 20 minutes or
until golden brown. Cool on wire racks. Store in an airtight container.

Michael Nelaborige
Vera Bradley Marketing Assistant

Caramel Layer Chocolate Squares

YIELD: 3 DOZEN

When I have a request for brownies, I always make this recipe
and no one is ever disappointed. They are fabulous.

1 (14-ounce) package caramels
  (about 50)
1/3 cup evaporated milk
1 (2-layer) package German
  chocolate cake mix

3/4 cup (1 1/2 sticks) butter, melted
1/3 cup evaporated milk
2 cups chocolate chips
1 cup pecans, chopped (optional)

Melt the caramels with 1/3 cup evaporated milk in a saucepan over low heat,
stirring constantly. Remove from heat.

Combine the cake mix, butter and 1/3 cup evaporated milk in a medium
bowl. Mix with a wooden spoon until the dough holds together. Press 1/2 of the
dough over the bottom of a buttered and floured 9×13-inch baking pan. Bake at
350 degrees for 6 minutes. Remove from the oven. Sprinkle with the chocolate
chips and pecans. Pour the caramel mixture evenly over the pecan layer.
Crumble the remaining dough over the top. Bake for 18 minutes. Refrigerate
immediately after baking and chill for 30 minutes. Cut into squares.

Julie Clymer
Vera Bradley Shipping Team

Chocolate Chip Butter Cookies

YIELD: 3 DOZEN

1 cup (2 sticks) butter
1 1/2 teaspoons vanilla extract
2 cups flour

1/8 teaspoon salt
1 cup confectioners' sugar
1/2 to 1 cup miniature chocolate chips

Melt the butter in a saucepan. Stir in the vanilla. Cool slightly. Combine
the flour, salt and confectioners' sugar in a large mixing bowl. Add the butter
mixture and mix well. Stir in the chocolate chips. The mixture will be crumbly.
Shape the dough into 1-inch balls. Place 2 inches apart on an ungreased cookie
sheet. Flatten each ball with the bottom of a glass. Bake at 350 degrees for 8 to
10 minutes or until light brown. Cool on a wire rack.

Nancy Negus
The Blackboard
Jacksonville, Illinois

Peanut Butter Chocolate Brownies

YIELD: 3 DOZEN

This is a Fourth of July favorite. I make this every year to take to our annual family get-together. These brownies taste great warm and are a delicious picnic pleaser.

1 (2-layer) package yellow cake mix
1 cup peanut butter
1/2 cup (1 stick) margarine, melted
2 eggs
1 cup chocolate chips

1 (14-ounce) can sweetened
  condensed milk
2 tablespoons margarine
1 (16-ounce) can pecan frosting

Combine the cake mix, peanut butter, 1/2 cup margarine and eggs in a large mixing bowl and mix well. Spread 2/3 of the mixture in an ungreased 9×13-inch baking pan.

Combine the chocolate chips, condensed milk, 2 tablespoons margarine and pecan frosting in a large saucepan. Cook over medium heat until melted. Pour into the prepared pan. Drop the remaining dough in big chunks over the filling. Bake at 350 degrees for 20 to 25 minutes or until the edges pull from the sides of the pan. Cut into squares.

Stacie Gray
Vera Bradley Customer Service

Ballpark Chocolate Chip Cookies

YIELD: 2 1/2 DOZEN

The vanilla pudding in the mix really makes these cookies moist.

1 cup (2 sticks) butter, softened
1/4 cup sugar
3/4 cup packed brown sugar
1 (4-ounce) package vanilla instant
  pudding mix

2 eggs
1 teaspoon vanilla extract
2 1/2 cups flour
1 teaspoon baking soda
2 cups chocolate chips

Cream the butter, sugar and brown sugar in a mixing bowl until light and fluffy. Add the pudding mix, eggs and vanilla and beat well. Beat in the flour and baking soda. Fold in the chocolate chips. Drop by teaspoonfuls onto an ungreased cookie sheet. Bake at 350 degrees for 7 to 10 minutes or until light brown on the top and edge; watch carefully to prevent overbrowning. You may use 1/2 cup (1 stick) margarine for 1/2 cup (1 stick) of the butter.

Ellen Pyle
Vera Bradley Classic Steering Committee

Kiffle Cups

YIELD: 4 DOZEN

They look and taste like miniature pecan pies. They are especially good around the holidays as a different Christmas cookie.

2 cups flour
1 cup (2 sticks) butter, softened
8 ounces cream cheese, softened
2 eggs
1 1/2 cups packed brown sugar

2 tablespoons butter or margarine,
  melted
2 teaspoons vanilla extract
1/8 teaspoon salt
1 1/3 cups chopped pecans

Combine the flour, butter and cream cheese in a small bowl and mix well using a wooden spoon. Shape into small balls about 3/4 inch in diameter. Press into miniature muffin cups to form shells.

Combine the eggs, brown sugar, butter, vanilla and salt in a bowl and mix well. Stir in the pecans. Fill the prepared muffin cups about 3/4 full. Bake at 400 degrees for 10 to 12 minutes.

Leslie K. Byrne
Daughter-in-law of Barbara Bradley Baekgaard

Lemon Pecan Wafers

YIELD: 6 DOZEN

2 cups flour
1 teaspoon baking powder
1/8 teaspoon salt
1/2 cup (1 stick) butter, softened
1 cup sugar

1 egg
1 tablespoon lemon zest
1 tablespoon fresh lemon juice
1 cup pecans, chopped, toasted

Mix the flour, baking powder and salt together. Cream the butter and sugar in a large mixing bowl until light and fluffy. Beat in the egg, lemon zest and lemon juice. Add the flour mixture gradually, beating constantly. Fold in the pecans.

Shape the dough into 2 rolls 1 1/2 inches in diameter. Wrap in waxed paper. Chill for 2 hours or until firm.

Unwrap the dough. Cut into 1/8-inch slices using a sharp knife. Place 1 inch apart on a greased cookie sheet. Bake at 375 degrees for 12 minutes or until the edges are light brown. Cool on a wire rack.

Becky Bennett
Vera Bradley Product Development Team

Spicy Oatmeal Cookies

YIELD: 2 DOZEN

1 1/2 cups flour
2 teaspoons ground cinnamon
2 teaspoons ground allspice
2 teaspoons ground cloves
1 teaspoon ground ginger
1/2 teaspoon baking soda
1/2 teaspoon salt

1 cup (2 sticks) butter, softened
1 cup sugar
1 cup packed brown sugar
2 eggs
1 teaspoon vanilla extract
3 cups quick-cooking oats
2 cups raisins (optional)

Mix the flour, cinnamon, allspice, cloves, ginger, baking soda and salt together. Cream the butter, sugar and brown sugar in a large mixing bowl until light and fluffy. Beat in the eggs and vanilla. Stir in the flour mixture. Fold in the oats and raisins. Let stand at room temperature for 2 hours.

Drop by tablespoonfuls onto a lightly greased cookie sheet. Flatten slightly with the back of a wet spoon or the bottom of a glass. Bake at 375 degrees for 10 minutes. Do not overbake. Remove from the oven. Cool on the cookie sheet for 1 to 2 minutes. Remove to a wire rack to cool completely.

Barbara Bradley Baekgaard
President and Co-Founder of Vera Bradley

Pumpkin Cookies

YIELD: 4 DOZEN

These are great for the kids to decorate into their favorite
pumpkin shapes or monster faces.

4 cups flour
2 cups rolled oats
2 teaspoons baking soda
2 teaspoons cinnamon
1 teaspoon salt
1¹/2 cups (3 sticks) margarine,
  softened

2 cups packed brown sugar
1 cup sugar
1 egg
1 teaspoon vanilla extract
1 (16-ounce) can solid-pack pumpkin
1 cup chocolate chips

Mix the flour, oats, baking soda, cinnamon and salt in a bowl. Cream the
margarine, brown sugar and sugar in a large mixing bowl until light and fluffy.
Add the egg, vanilla and pumpkin. Add the flour mixture 1/3 at a time, beating
well after each addition. Fold in the chocolate chips. Drop by teaspoonfuls onto
an ungreased cookie sheet. Flatten with the back of a fork. Bake at 350 degrees
for 14 minutes. Cool on a wire rack. You may decorate with orange and green
frostings to make the cookies look like pumpkins, or decorate as you wish.

Leslie K. Byrne
Daughter-in-law of Barbara Bradley Baekgaard

Buttermilk Sugar Cookies

YIELD: 4 TO 5 DOZEN

If you have been looking for the recipe for the sugar cookies
from your favorite bakery, here it is.

4 to 5 cups flour
2 teaspoons baking soda
1 teaspoon salt
1 cup shortening

2 cups sugar
2 eggs
1 cup buttermilk
2 teaspoons vanilla extract

Mix 4 cups flour, baking soda and salt together. Cream the shortening and
sugar in a mixing bowl until light and fluffy. Beat in the eggs. Add the flour
mixture alternately with the buttermilk, beating constantly. Stir in the vanilla.
Add enough of the remaining flour to make of the desired consistency.

   Roll out on a floured surface. Cut into desired shapes. Place on a nonstick
cookie sheet. Bake at 325 degrees for 7 to 10 minutes or until golden brown.

Julie Clymer
Vera Bradley Shipping Team

Pink Chinchilla Pie

Try this pie as a refreshing summertime dessert.

2 cups shredded coconut
2 tablespoons butter, melted
1/2 gallon French vanilla ice cream,
    softened

6 tablespoons crème de noyaux
3 tablespoons crème de cacao

Combine the coconut and butter in a bowl and mix well. Pat over the bottom and up the side of a 10-inch pie plate. Bake at 350 degrees for 10 minutes or until golden brown. Watch carefully. The coconut can burn easily and quickly.

Combine the ice cream and liqueurs in a bowl and mix well. Spoon into the baked pie shell. Freeze until firm. Garnish with strawberries, slivered almonds and whipped cream.

Pat Kramer
Letter Perfect at the Balcony
Schenectady, New York

Pumpkin Pecan Pie

This is the pie for those people who would like to have
"a small piece of each" . . . pumpkin and pecan.

1 egg, lightly beaten
1 cup cooked or canned pumpkin
1/3 cup sugar
1 tablespoon pumpkin pie spice
1 unbaked (9-inch) pie shell
2/3 cup light corn syrup

2 eggs
1/2 cup sugar
3 tablespoons butter, melted
1/2 teaspoon vanilla extract
1 cup pecan halves

Combine the egg, pumpkin, 1/3 cup sugar and pumpkin pie spice in a medium mixing bowl and mix well. Spread in the unbaked pie shell. Combine the corn syrup, 2 eggs, 1/2 cup sugar, butter and vanilla in a bowl and mix well. Stir in the pecans. Spoon over the pumpkin layer. Bake at 350 degrees for 50 minutes.

Jill Nichols
Vera Bradley Executive Vice President/COO

Honey Pecan Pie

1 cup flour	1/3 cup sugar
1/2 teaspoon salt	1/3 cup packed brown sugar
1/2 cup shortening	3 eggs, lightly beaten
1/4 cup (about) cold water	1/4 cup (1/2 stick) butter, melted
1/2 cup honey	1 teaspoon vanilla extract
1/2 cup white corn syrup	1 cup pecan halves

Process the flour, salt and shortening in a food processor until combined. Add enough of the cold water in a fine stream to form a ball, processing constantly. Wrap the ball in plastic wrap. Chill for 1 hour or longer. Unwrap the dough. Roll into a 10-inch circle on a lightly floured surface. Fit into a 9-inch pie plate, trimming and fluting the edge.

Combine the honey, corn syrup, sugar, brown sugar, eggs, butter and vanilla in a large mixing bowl and mix well. Spoon into the prepared pie plate. Arrange the pecans on the filling, covering completely. Bake at 375 degrees for 40 to 50 minutes or until the filling is set and the crust is golden brown. Cool on a wire rack for 20 minutes or longer. Serve cold or slightly warmed with whipped cream.

Katie Burns
Friend of Vera Bradley Designs

Chocolate Caramel Tart

YIELD: 8 SERVINGS

For the true chocolate lover—it's fantastic.

1 cup flour	3/4 cup heavy cream
3 tablespoons sugar	1 cup semisweet chocolate chips
1 teaspoon lemon zest	3/4 cup sugar
1/8 teaspoon salt	1/3 cup water
1/2 cup (1 stick) unsalted butter, cut into 1/2-inch pieces	1/3 cup heavy cream
	5 tablespoons unsalted butter, softened
1 egg yolk	1 teaspoon vanilla extract
1/2 teaspoon vanilla extract	1/8 teaspoon salt

Blend the flour, 3 tablespoons sugar, lemon zest and 1/8 teaspoon salt in a food processor for 5 seconds. Add 1/2 cup butter, egg yolk and 1/2 teaspoon vanilla. Process until a large moist clump forms. Shape into a ball and knead briefly to combine. Flatten into a disk. Wrap in plastic wrap. Chill for 30 minutes or until firm enough to roll out.

Roll the dough between 2 sheets of plastic wrap into a 12-inch circle. Peel off the top sheet of plastic wrap. Turn the dough over and press into a 9-inch tart pan with a removable bottom. Peel off the plastic wrap. Fold in the excess dough, forming double-thick sides. Prick the shell all over with a fork. Freeze for 15 minutes. Bake at 400 degrees for 10 minutes. Press the shell flat using the back of a fork if the bottom bubbles. Bake for 10 minutes longer or until the crust is golden brown. Cool on a wire rack.

Bring 3/4 cup cream to a boil in a heavy small saucepan. Remove from heat. Add the chocolate chips and whisk until smooth. Spread 1 cup of the chocolate filling into the piecrust. Chill for 45 minutes or until firm. Reserve the remaining chocolate filling in the saucepan.

Combine 3/4 cup sugar and the water in a heavy medium saucepan. Heat over low heat until the sugar dissolves, stirring constantly. Increase heat. Boil for 8 minutes or until the syrup is amber color. Brush down the side with a wet pastry brush and swirl the pan occasionally. Remove from heat. Add 1/3 cup cream, 5 tablespoons butter, 1 teaspoon vanilla and 1/8 teaspoon salt. The mixture will bubble. Cook over low heat for 5 minutes or until smooth and the color deepens, stirring constantly. Chill for 20 minutes or until cold but not firm. Spoon over the chocolate layer. Pipe or drizzle the reserved chocolate filling decoratively over the caramel. Chill for 1 hour or until the caramel is firm.

Patti Pine
Vera Bradley Sales Representative Coordinator

Contributors

Nancy Adams
Lou Alexander
Palma Ashley
Barbara B. Baekgaard
Diane Barnes
Jane Barrick
Becky Bennett
Lee Ann Berning
Helen Bigg
A. Kay Black
Kathy Blackman
Debra Bleeke
Cher Bond
Joan Bond
Melodie Botteron
Vera Bradley
Joan Bradley Reedy
Sue Britton
Diane Brown
Monica Brown
Stacey Sloan Brown
Susie Bruce
Amy Bryan
Katie Burns
Pamela Butler-Channel
Leslie K. Byrne
Joanie Byrne Hall
Allie Carmack
Lisa Cashel
Mary Ellen Casson
Mike and Maureen Catalogna
Chip Chevillet
Stefanie Chevillet
Will Cleveland
Julie Clymer

Kim Colby
Mercedes Cox
Carolyn Davis
Jolene Doyle
Nancy Ecclestone
Troy Edgington
Barb Erhardt
Debbie Ferguson
Renee Fitch
LeAnn Frankle
Betty Genter
Donna Gentile
David Goodman
Cindy Graham
Nancy Graham
Mary Ann Gray
Stacie Gray
Amy Grinsfelder
Dede Hall
Betsy Lewis Harned
Mary Harper
Karen Hazelett
Ruth Henderson
Skitch Henderson
Mary Jo Hetrick
Eda Holt
Betty Howell
Jane Jarvis
Dot Johnson
Eddie Johnson
Marta Johnson
Phil Johnson
Katrina Kay
Jennifer Kennedy
Sharon Keogh

Lyn Killoran
Doris Knaus
Pat Kramer
Cheri Lantz
Rita LeFavour
Cookie Leiber
Darcie Lentz
Phyllis Loy
Vi MacMurdo
Pat Mallery
Dana Manning
Melanie Mauger
Dorothy McAfee
Connie McNamara
Amy Merselis
Michelle Meullion
Bonnie Stewart Mickelson
Kathy Miller
Patricia R. Miller
Denise Mitchell
Karen Moore
Nancy Negus
Marilyn Neil
Michael Nelaborige
Joyce Neubauer
Jill Nichols
Jennifer Parker
Debbie Peterson
Mimi Phillips
Patti Pine
Nancy Pishney
Pat Polito
Lila Pursley
Ellen Pyle
Jean Quinn

Amy Ray
Kathy Reedy Ray
Mike Ray
Kerry Reedy
Patti Reedy
Glenna Reno
Sue Reynen
Emilie Robertson
Susan Sandlin
Sandy Schelm
Mari Belle Severine
May Shearon
Kitch Somers
Ginger Stockton
Gail Tate
Regina Thibideau
Nieta Van Engelenhoven
Mary Beth Wahl
Jeannine Wallace
Barbara Weber
Rosie Welsh
Debbie Wilson
Judy Wintin
Nan Yablong
Jim Yerrick
Thirza Youker
Deb Young
Wendy Young
Dan's Tog Shop
Misericordia Gift Shop
The Depot, New Jersey

Index

Accompaniments. *See also* Garnishes; Sauces
Garlic Basil Mayonnaise, 152
Onion Jalapeño Marmalade, 113

Appetizers. *See also* Dips; Snacks; Spreads
Appetizer Steak Kabobs, 45
Artichoke Phyllo Flowers, 44
Baked Brie with Caramelized Onions and
Tomato Preserves, 41
Baked Chèvre with Sun-Dried Tomatoes and
Basil, 43
Caviar Pie, 43
Chili Brie in Sourdough, 42
Kathleen's Marinated Shrimp, 41
Mediterranean Pizza, 46
Red Pepper and Goat Cheese
Pizza, 47
Vickki's Hors d'Oeuvre, 45

Apple
Applesauce Jumbles, 190
Apple Strudel Bars, 15
Aunt Franny's Apple Cake, 173

Artichokes
Artichoke Phyllo Flowers, 44
Colorado Pasta Salad, 87
Hearty Mediterranean Torte, 153
Mediterranean Pizza, 46
Mushroom and Artichoke Soup, 57
Red Pepper and Goat Cheese Pizza, 47

Asparagus
Asparagus Salad, 72
Fresh Spring Asparagus, 86
Italian Veggie Burgers, 152

Avocado
Chicken and Corn Tostada Salad, 82
Mexican Fiesta Salad, 80
Shrimp and Pasta Salad with Tomatoes and
Avocado, 85

Bacon
Calico Beans, 88
Cashew Pea Salad, 74
Chip's Grilled Potatoes, 94
Clam Chowder, 68
Classic Beef Stew, 109
Hoosier Corn Pudding, 90
Mexican Fiesta Salad, 80
Sausage and Bean Casserole, 117
Spinach Salad with Hot Bacon Raspberry
Vinaigrette, 78
Warm Bleu Cheese, Bacon and Garlic Dip, 33
Warm Swiss Cheese and Bacon Dip, 36

Banana
Banana Split Dessert, 159
Hummingbird Cake, 180
Traditional Banana Bread with
Pecans, 21

Beef. *See also* Ground Beef; Veal
Appetizer Steak Kabobs, 45
Beef with Shrimp, 106
Braised Beef, 108
Classic Beef Stew, 109
Forgotten Roast, 108
Marinated Flank Steak, 107
Tabasco Seared Rib-Eye Steaks, 107

Beverages, Cold
Champagne Punch, 50
Eggnog, 49
Grapefruit Margaritas, 50
Sparkling Raspberry Lemonade, 51
Sunny Day Sangria, 49

Beverages, Hot
Hot Cranberry Tea, 53
Irish Crème, 52
Santa's Cocoa Mix, 52
Warm Spiced Tea, 53

Black Beans
Black Bean Hummus, 32
Black Bean Toss, 32
Chicken and Corn Tostada Salad, 82
Chicken Chili, 64
Mexican Fiesta Salad, 80
Tortilla Black Bean Casserole, 149

Blueberry
Blueberry Muffins Supreme, 17
Lemon Blueberry Bread, 22
Mixed Berry Crisp, 160

Breads. *See also* Coffee Cakes; Rolls; Waffles
Blueberry Muffins Supreme, 17
Boston Brown Bread, 26
French Bread with Herb Butter, 27
French Bread with Pesto Parmesan
Spread, 27
Irish Soda Bread, 25
Lemon Blueberry Bread, 22
Pumpkin Tea Bread, 23
Traditional Banana Bread with
Pecans, 21
Zucchini Bread, 24

Broccoli
Broccoli Pesto, 87
Nora's Broccoli and Carrot Casserole, 89

Brownies
Caramel Layer Chocolate Squares, 192
Peanut Butter Chocolate Brownies, 193

Cabbage
Chinese Coleslaw, 77
Danish Red Cabbage, 89
Super Slaw, 77
Vera's Beefy Vegetable Soup, 60
Wish'n Well Chicken Soup, 67

Cakes
Aunt Franny's Apple Cake, 173
Bourbon Chocolate Pecan Cake, 179
Chiffon Cake with Citrus Sauce, 175
Chocolate Mint Squares, 177
Hummingbird Cake, 180
Nectarine Coconut Cake, 176
Orange Blossom Bridesmaid Luncheon
    Cake, 181
Pecan Pie Cake, 182
Pumpkin Roll with Toffee Cream Filling and
    Caramel Sauce, 184
Ruth's Italian Pound Cake, 185
Sloppy Pineapple Cake, 186
Traditional Carrot Cake, 174
Triple-Chocolate Layer Cake, 178
Vanilla Butter and Nut Cake, 188
Vera's Yum-Yum Cake, 187

Cakes, Fillings
Pecan Pie Cake Filling, 183
Toffee Cream Filling, 185

Candy
Joel's Award-Winning Fudge, 189
Praline Grahams, 189

Carrots
Chicken Soup with Ricotta Dumplings, 65
Chunky Minestrone, 62
Classic Beef Stew, 109
Eight-Vegetable Marinated Salad, 79
Grocery Shopper's Soup, 60
Nora's Broccoli and Carrot Casserole, 89
Potato Salad, 75
Southwest Roasted Red Pepper Bisque, 56
Super Slaw, 77
Traditional Carrot Cake, 174
Tucson Soup, 61
Vera's Beefy Vegetable Soup, 60
Wish'n Well Chicken Soup, 67

Cheesecakes
Candy Bar Cheesecake, 162
Lemon Swirl Cheesecake, 163
Rosebud's Cheesecake Supreme, 164

Chicken
Almond Cherry Chicken Salad, 81
Baked Pineapple Chicken, 121
Chicken and Corn Tostada Salad, 82
Chicken and Wild Rice Casserole, 126
Chicken Chili, 64
Chicken Elizabeth, 118
Chicken Piccata, 119
Chicken Soup with Ricotta Dumplings, 65
Creamy Chicken and Tomato
    Casserole, 144
Curried Chicken Salad, 83
Grandma Beebe's Chicken Casserole, 123
Grilled Chicken, 117
Killer White Chili, 65
Lila's Chicken, 122
MAC's Chicken and Ham Casserole, 124
Nutty Chicken Casserole, 125
Orange Cashew Chicken Salad, 84
Pasta with Sausage and Chicken, 143

Roasted Whole Lemon Chickens, 120
Sesame Chicken Kabobs, 121
Swiss Chicken Casserole, 125
Tortilla Black Bean Casserole, 149
White Lasagna, 137
Wildwood's Famous Chicken Tortilla
    Soup, 66
Wish'n Well Chicken Soup, 67

Chili
Chicken Chili, 64
Killer White Chili, 65
Mom's Chili, 63

Chocolate
All-American Peppermint Stick Torte with
    Fudge Topping, 170
Ballpark Chocolate Chip Cookies, 194
"Better than Martha's" Chocolate Waffles
    with Boysenberry Sauce, 166
Bourbon Chocolate Pecan Cake, 179
Candy Bar Cheesecake, 162
Caramel Layer Chocolate Squares, 192
Chocolate and Peanut Butter Dessert, 167
Chocolate Caramel Tart, 199
Chocolate Chip Butter Cookies, 192
Chocolate Glaze, 177, 179
Chocolate Mint Squares, 177
Chocolate Mousse Cake, 165
Death by Chocolate, 165
Éclair Torte, 171
Irish Crème, 52
Joel's Award-Winning Fudge, 189
Layered Mocha Cream Torte, 169
Peanut Butter Chocolate Brownies, 193
Pumpkin Cookies, 196
Santa's Cocoa Mix, 52
Triple-Chocolate Layer Cake, 178

Clams
Clam Chowder, 68
Clam Dip, 39

Coffee Cakes
Apple Strudel Bars, 15
Danish Puffs, 18
Delicious Coffee Cake, 19
Raspberry Cream Cheese Coffee Cake, 20
Sunday-Best Coffee Cake, 19

Cookies. *See also* Brownies
Applesauce Jumbles, 190
Ballpark Chocolate Chip Cookies, 194
Buttermilk Sugar Cookies, 196
Chocolate Chip Butter Cookies, 192
Cinnamon and Sugar Biscotti, 191
Kiffle Cups, 194
Lemon Pecan Wafers, 195
Pumpkin Cookies, 196
Spicy Oatmeal Cookies, 195

Corn
Black Bean Toss, 32
Chicken and Corn Tostada Salad, 82
Chicken Chili, 64
Connoisseur's Casserole, 100
Eight-Vegetable Marinated Salad, 79

Fresh Corn Chowder, 57
Hoosier Corn Pudding, 90
Mexican Fiesta Salad, 80
Roasted Red Pepper, Corn and Rice Salad, 76
Southern Succotash, 100

Cranberry
Cranberry Sauce with Apricots and
 Raisins, 103
Hot Cranberry Tea, 53
Sunny Day Sangria, 49

Desserts. *See also* Cakes; Candy; Cheesecakes;
 Cookies; Pies; Sauces, Dessert
All-American Peppermint Stick Torte with
 Fudge Topping, 170
Banana Split Dessert, 159
Berry-Filled Meringue Hearts, 161
"Better than Martha's" Chocolate Waffles
 with Boysenberry Sauce, 166
Chocolate and Peanut Butter Dessert, 167
Chocolate Mousse Cake, 165
Death by Chocolate, 165
Easy Baklava, 158
Éclair Torte, 171
Kimberly's Pumpkin Cake Dessert, 168
Layered Mocha Cream Torte, 169
Mixed Berry Crisp, 160
Strawberry Custard, 172

Dips
Beer Cheese Dip, 35
Black Bean Hummus, 32
Black Bean Toss, 32
Clam Dip, 39
Crowd-Pleasing Taco Dip, 37
Millie's Curried Dip, 38
Roasted Red Pepper Dip, 36
Smoked Salmon Dip, 40
The Ultimate Crab Dip, 39
Warm Bleu Cheese, Bacon and Garlic
 Dip, 33
Warm Swiss Cheese and Bacon Dip, 36
White Mexican Cheese Dip, 35

Egg Dishes
Crustless Swiss Quiches, 11
Italian Strata, 13
Sausage Cheese Strata with Sun-Dried
 Tomatoes, 14
Scalloped Eggs and Cheese, 10
Soufflé of Goat Cheese with Smoked Salmon
 and Dill, 12

Fish. *See also* Salmon
Jalapeño Grilled Fish, 130
Lemon Stuffed Sole Fillets, 134
Smoked White Fish Pâté, 40

Frostings
Butter and Nut Frosting, 188
Cream Cheese Frosting, 16, 174, 180
Pecan Cream Cheese Frosting, 186

Garnishes
Candied Orange Peel, 181
Pastry Leaves and Pecans, 183

Glazes
Brandy Glaze, 173
Browned Butter Glaze, 190
Chocolate Glaze, 177, 179
Confectioners' Sugar Glaze, 18
Lemon Glaze, 22

Green Beans
Calico Beans, 88
Connoisseur's Casserole, 100
Eight-Vegetable Marinated Salad, 79
Green Bean and New Potato Salad, 74
Tomato and Green Bean Risotto with Feta
 Cheese, 98

Ground Beef
California Patty Melts, 150
Chile Relleno Casserole, 110
Crowd-Pleasing Taco Dip, 37
Mexican Meat Loaf, 111
Mom's Chili, 63
Sombrero Spread, 37
South-of-the-Border Lasagna, 139
Spaghetti Sauce, 141
Stroganoff Casserole, 142
Vera's Beefy Vegetable Soup, 60
World's Best Lasagna, 138

Ham
Hearty Mediterranean Torte, 153
Jambalaya Pasta, 140
MAC's Chicken and Ham Casserole, 124

Lamb
Stuffed Leg of Lamb, 112

Lasagna
South-of-the-Border Lasagna, 139
White Lasagna, 137
World's Best Lasagna, 138

Lemon
Champagne Punch, 50
Hot Cranberry Tea, 53
Lemon Blueberry Bread, 22
Lemon Glaze, 22
Lemon Pecan Wafers, 195
Lemon Stuffed Sole Fillets, 134
Lemon Swirl Cheesecake, 163
Roasted Whole Lemon Chickens, 120
Sparkling Raspberry Lemonade, 51
Sunny Day Sangria, 49
Warm Spiced Tea, 53

Lime
Baked Salmon on a Bed of Leeks, 131
Cilantro Lime Vinaigrette, 85
Citrus-Marinated Turkey Breast, 127
Curry-Crusted Shrimp with Cilantro and
 Lime, 136
Grapefruit Margaritas, 50
Grilled Garlic Lime Pork Tenderloin, 113

Mushrooms
Braised Beef, 108
Chicken and Wild Rice Casserole, 126
Chicken Piccata, 119

Classic Beef Stew, 109
Creamy Mushroom Bake, 92
Hearty Mediterranean Torte, 153
Hearty Tortellini Vegetable Soup, 63
Italian Veggie Burgers, 152
Lila's Chicken, 122
MAC's Chicken and Ham Casserole, 124
Mom's Traditional Stuffing, 129
Mushroom and Artichoke Soup, 57
Mushroom Gravy, 129
Sautéed Spinach with Mushrooms, 97
Spaghetti Pie, 141
Spinach Salad with Hot Bacon Raspberry
    Vinaigrette, 78
Stroganoff Casserole, 142
Wild Mushroom Bread Pudding, 91

Onions
Baked Vidalia Onions, 92
Cheesy Onion Casserole, 93
Swiss Onion Soup, 58

Orange
Candied Orange Peel, 181
Champagne Punch, 50
Citrus-Marinated Turkey Breast, 127
Cranberry Sauce with Apricots and
    Raisins, 103
Fresh Orange Vinaigrette, 69
Hot Cranberry Tea, 53
Mandarin Orange and Lettuce Salad, 70
Orange Blossom Bridesmaid Luncheon
    Cake, 181
Orange Cashew Chicken Salad, 84
Sunny Day Sangria, 49
Sweet-and-Sour Dressing, 84
Warm Spiced Tea, 53

Pasta. *See also* Lasagna; Salads, Pasta
Carolina Oregano Shrimp, 145
Chunky Minestrone, 62
Creamy Chicken and Tomato Casserole, 144
Hearty Tortellini Vegetable Soup, 63
Jambalaya Pasta, 140
Lila's Chicken, 122
Pasta with Fresh Tomato Sauce, 148
Pasta with Sausage and Chicken, 143
Roasted Bell Pepper Pasta, 147
Shrimp in Angel Hair Pasta, 146
Spaghetti Pie, 141
Stroganoff Casserole, 142
Tucson Soup, 61

Pear
Pear, Watercress and Endive Salad with Sweet
    Gorgonzola, 71
Salad with Pears, Walnuts and Bleu
    Cheese, 71

Pesto
Broccoli Pesto, 87
Sunflower Seed Pesto, 34

Pies
Caviar Pie, 43
Chocolate Caramel Tart, 199
Honey Pecan Pie, 198

Pink Chinchilla Pie, 197
Pumpkin Pecan Pie, 197

Pineapple
Baked Pineapple Chicken, 121
Banana Split Dessert, 159
Hummingbird Cake, 180
Sloppy Pineapple Cake, 186

Pizza
Mediterranean Pizza, 46
Red Pepper and Goat Cheese Pizza, 47

Pork. *See also* Bacon; Ham; Sausage
Barbecued Pork Sandwiches, 154
Grilled Garlic Lime Pork Tenderloin, 113
Jerk Pork, 116
Mexican Meat Loaf, 111
Pork Chop Casserole, 116
Pork Crown Roast with Gravy, 115
Pork Medallions in Creamy Mustard
    Sauce, 114
Vera's Glazed Pork Roast, 114
Wild Rice Stuffing, 115

Potatoes
Chip's Grilled Potatoes, 94
Clam Chowder, 68
Easy Cheesy Spuds, 93
Forgotten Roast, 108
Fresh Corn Chowder, 57
Garlic Mashed Red Potatoes, 94
Green Bean and New Potato Salad, 74
Grocery Shopper's Soup, 60
Make-Ahead Mashed Potatoes, 95
Potato Cheese Soup, 59
Potato Salad, 75
Shredded Parmesan Potatoes, 95
Tucson Soup, 61
Twice-Baked Potatoes, 96
Vera's Beefy Vegetable Soup, 60

Poultry. *See* Chicken; Turkey

Pumpkin
Kimberly's Pumpkin Cake Dessert, 168
Pumpkin Cookies, 196
Pumpkin Pecan Pie, 197
Pumpkin Roll with Toffee Cream Filling and
    Caramel Sauce, 184
Pumpkin Tea Bread, 23

Raspberry
Berry-Filled Meringue Hearts, 161
Boysenberry Sauce, 167
Mixed Berry Crisp, 160
Pistachio-Crusted Goat Cheese with Fresh
    Orange Vinaigrette, 69
Raspberry Cream Cheese Coffee Cake, 20
Sparkling Raspberry Lemonade, 49
Spinach Salad with Hot Bacon Raspberry
    Vinaigrette, 78

Rice
Champagne Shrimp, 135
Chicken and Wild Rice Casserole, 126
Grandma Beebe's Chicken Casserole, 123

Nutty Chicken Casserole, 125
Pork Chop Casserole, 116
Roasted Red Pepper, Corn and Rice Salad, 76
Southwest Roasted Red Pepper Bisque, 56
Tomato and Green Bean Risotto with Feta
    Cheese, 98
Wild Rice Stuffing, 115

Rolls
Best-Ever Cinnamon Rolls, 16
Out-of-this-World Rolls, 28
Sesame Holiday Rolls, 29

Salad Dressings
Cilantro Lime Vinaigrette, 85
Cilantro Vinaigrette, 81
Curried Mayonnaise, 83
Fresh Orange Vinaigrette, 69
Sweet-and-Sour Dressing, 84
Vinaigrette, 70

Salads
Almond Cherry Chicken Salad, 81
Chicken and Corn Tostada Salad, 82
Curried Chicken Salad, 83
Orange Cashew Chicken Salad, 84

Salads, Fruit
Mandarin Orange and Lettuce Salad, 70
Pear, Watercress and Endive Salad with Sweet
    Gorgonzola, 71
Pistachio-Crusted Goat Cheese with Fresh
    Orange Vinaigrette, 69
Salad with Pears, Walnuts and Bleu
    Cheese, 71
Salad with Strawberries and Almonds, 72

Salads, Pasta
Colorado Pasta Salad, 87
Pasta Salad with Basil, Sungold Cherry
    Tomatoes and Goat Cheese, 86
Shrimp and Pasta Salad with Tomatoes and
    Avocado, 85

Salads, Vegetable
Asparagus Salad, 72
Caesar Salad, 73
Cashew Pea Salad, 74
Chinese Coleslaw, 77
Eight-Vegetable Marinated Salad, 79
Green Bean and New Potato Salad, 74
Mexican Fiesta Salad, 80
Potato Salad, 75
Radish Salad, 78
Roasted Red Pepper, Corn and Rice Salad, 76
Spinach Salad with Hot Bacon Raspberry
    Vinaigrette, 78
Super Slaw, 77
Wine Lovers' Salad, 79

Salmon
Baked Salmon on a Bed of Leeks, 131
Foxy Loxburgers, 133
Pacific Salmon Loaf, 133
Poached Salmon, 130
Salmon Napoleon, 132
Smoked Salmon Dip, 40

Soufflé of Goat Cheese with Smoked Salmon
    and Dill, 12
Spice-Crusted Salmon with Salsa, 132

Sandwiches
Barbecued Pork Sandwiches, 154
California Patty Melts, 150
Foxy Loxburgers, 133
Hearty Mediterranean Torte, 153
Herbed Vegetable Sandwiches with
    Anchovies, 155
Italian Veggie Burgers, 152
Spinach Feta Burgers, 151

Sauces
Brown Sauce, 112
Light Cheese Sauce, 90
Mushroom Gravy, 129
Roasted Tomato and Garlic Sauce, 99
Spaghetti Sauce, 141
White Wine Sauce, 118

Sauces, Dessert
Boysenberry Sauce, 167
Citrus Sauce, 175
Walloon Lake Inn's Grand Marnier
    Sabayon Sauce, 172

Sausage
Chicken and Wild Rice
    Casserole, 126
Grocery Shopper's Soup, 60
Italian Strata, 13
Jambalaya Pasta, 140
Pasta with Sausage and Chicken, 143
Sausage and Bean Casserole, 117
Sausage Cheese Strata with Sun-Dried
    Tomatoes, 14
Spaghetti Pie, 141
World's Best Lasagna, 138

Seafood. *See also* Clams; Fish; Shrimp
The Ultimate Crab Dip, 39

Shrimp
Beef with Shrimp, 106
Carolina Oregano Shrimp, 145
Champagne Shrimp, 135
Colorado Pasta Salad, 87
Curry-Crusted Shrimp with Cilantro
    and Lime, 136
Gulf Shrimp Beer Boil, 137
Jambalaya Pasta, 140
Kathleen's Marinated Shrimp, 41
Shrimp and Pasta Salad with Tomatoes
    and Avocado, 85
Shrimp in Angel Hair Pasta, 146

Side Dishes. *See also* Rice
Cold Sun-Dried Tomato and Feta Soufflé, 99
Cranberry Sauce with Apricots and
    Raisins, 103
Creamy Mushroom Bake, 92
Hoosier Corn Pudding, 90
Mom's Traditional Stuffing, 129
Southwestern-Style Corn Bread
    Dressing, 101

Tomato and Green Bean Risotto with
    Feta Cheese, 98
Wild Mushroom Bread Pudding, 91
Wild Rice Stuffing, 115

Snacks
Frog Mix, 48
Spicy Pecans, 48

Soups
Chicken Soup with Ricotta
    Dumplings, 65
Chunky Minestrone, 62
Clam Chowder, 68
Classic Beef Stew, 109
Fresh Corn Chowder, 57
Grocery Shopper's Soup, 60
Hearty Tortellini Vegetable Soup, 63
Mushroom and Artichoke Soup, 57
Potato Cheese Soup, 59
Southwest Roasted Red Pepper
    Bisque, 56
Squash Soup, 59
Swiss Onion Soup, 58
Tucson Soup, 61
Vera's Beefy Vegetable Soup, 60
Wildwood's Famous Chicken Tortilla
    Soup, 66
Wish'n Well Chicken Soup, 67

Spinach
Chunky Minestrone, 62
Grocery Shopper's Soup, 60
Hearty Mediterranean Torte, 153
Hearty Tortellini Vegetable Soup, 63
Italian Strata, 13
Red Pepper and Goat Cheese Pizza, 47
Salmon Napoleon, 132
Sautéed Spinach with Mushrooms, 97
Spinach Feta Burgers, 151
Spinach Salad with Hot Bacon Raspberry
    Vinaigrette, 78
Stuffed Leg of Lamb, 112
World's Best Lasagna, 138

Spreads
Curried Chutney Cheese Ball, 33
Smoked White Fish Pâté, 40
Sombrero Spread, 37
Tomato Pesto Cheese Mold, 34

Squash
Squash Soup, 59
Zucchini Gratin with Parmesan Cheese
    and Thyme, 102

Strata
Italian Strata, 13
Sausage Cheese Strata with Sun-Dried
    Tomatoes, 14

Strawberry
Banana Split Dessert, 159
Berry-Filled Meringue Hearts, 161
Champagne Punch, 50
Mixed Berry Crisp, 160
Salad with Strawberries and Almonds, 72

Strawberry Custard, 172
Vera's Yum-Yum Cake, 187
Walloon Lake Inn's Grand Marnier
    Sabayon Sauce, 172

Stuffings
Mom's Traditional Stuffing, 129
Wild Rice Stuffing, 115

Sun-Dried Tomatoes
Baked Chèvre with Sun-Dried Tomatoes and
    Basil, 43
Cold Sun-Dried Tomato and Feta Soufflé, 99
Creamy Chicken and Tomato Casserole, 144
Red Pepper and Goat Cheese Pizza, 47
Roasted Red Pepper Dip, 36
Sausage Cheese Strata with Sun-Dried
    Tomatoes, 14
Tomato and Green Bean Risotto with
    Feta Cheese, 98
Tomato Pesto Cheese Mold, 34

Tea
Hot Cranberry Tea, 53
Warm Spiced Tea, 53

Tortes
All-American Peppermint Stick Torte with
    Fudge Topping, 170
Éclair Torte, 171
Layered Mocha Cream Torte, 169

Turkey
Citrus-Marinated Turkey Breast, 127
Grilled Turkey with Stuffing and Mushroom
    Gravy, 128

Veal
Mexican Meat Loaf, 111

Vegetables. *See also* Artichokes; Asparagus;
    Black Beans; Broccoli; Cabbage; Carrots;
    Corn; Green Beans; Mushrooms; Onions;
    Potatoes; Salads, Vegetable; Spinach;
    Squash; Sun-Dried Tomatoes; Zucchini
Brandied Sweet Potatoes, 97
Calico Beans, 88
Connoisseur's Casserole, 100
Herbed Vegetable Sandwiches with
    Anchovies, 155
Italian Veggie Burgers, 152
Southern Succotash, 100

Waffles
"Better than Martha's" Chocolate Waffles
    with Boysenberry Sauce, 166
Crispy Waffles, 21

Zucchini
Chunky Minestrone, 62
Hearty Tortellini Vegetable Soup, 63
Herbed Vegetable Sandwiches with
    Anchovies, 155
Italian Strata, 13
Zucchini Bread, 24
Zucchini Gratin with Parmesan Cheese
    and Thyme, 102

Additional copies of this cookbook may be purchased from a Vera Bradley retailer.
To locate a retailer near you, visit our website at www.verabradley.com.